D0910225

ACKNOWLEDGMENT

The authors wish to thank Mr. Alfred P. Sheinwold for valuable advice and assistance in the preparation of this book.

Games For Two

By Albert H. Morehead and Geoffrey Mott-Smith

Introduction by Ely Culbertson

The John C. Winston Company
PHILADELPHIA   TORONTO

Copyright, 1947, by
THE JOHN C. WINSTON COMPANY

Copyright in Great Britain
and in the British Dominions
and Possessions

Copyright in the Philippines

Made in the United States of America

CONTENTS

INTRODUCTION

Four make a bridge game, but sometimes you haven't four players; and three's a crowd. So what to do? There are various solutions, one of which is to play two-hand games.

Among my oldest and most respected friends are Al Morehead and Geoff Mott-Smith. I know from long experience that any book by Morehead and Mott-Smith must be good. That makes this book the best possible answer to any question about "Games for Two." They have even told you how to play bridge for two, if you wish.

I must admit that my own favorite two-hand game is double solitaire. I suggested that they put it in. They pointed to Russian Bank, and refused. So I shall someday write a book about double solitaire. Until then, this is the book for me.

ELY CULBERTSON

RUMMY

Why You'll Like It: This is the best-known of all American games. Seventy million Americans play cards, and 49% of them know how to play Rummy. Originally it was a Spanish game (and before that it probably came from the Orient, as a form of Mah Jongg!), but its almost universal adoption in the United States showed that no other game is better suited to the American temperament. The most popular form of Rummy today is "Gin," which is explained on page 16.

What You Need: A standard 52-card pack, with pencil and paper for keeping score.

Let's Play a Game: You spread the pack on the table and you and your opponent each draw a card. His card is the ♦ 9 and yours the ♣ 9. That is a tie, because the suits have no ranking in Rummy, so you both draw again. This time he gets the ♠ A and you have the ♣ J. His card is lower—the ace always ranking below the deuce—and that means he has to deal first.

He shuffles the cards, you cut, and then he deals two hands of ten cards each, one at a time. The rest of the pack is placed face down on the table between you, making the *stock*. The top card of the stock is turned over and laid beside the stock. This starter proves to be the ♦ 10.

Your hand is

This arrangement in suits, however, is not convenient for Rummy. It is better to sort the cards by rank, or at least get all cards of the same or near rank together, thus

What you must try to do is to get all ten of your cards *matched* in some way. There are two kinds of groups of matched cards:

RUMMY

(a) Three or four of a kind, such as:

(b) A sequence of three or more in the same suit, such as ♥ Q J 10. Remember that ace is low, so that A-K-Q is not a sequence.

When you have such a matched set, you may *meld* it in any turn. Melding is simply laying the cards face up on the table in front of you. The first to meld all his cards will be the winner.

Your hand already contains a matched set, the three sixes. Every other card except the ♠ K is part of a combination—a group that can turn into a matched set by the addition of one card. That is, adding any one of the following cards to your hand would complete another set: ♠ 9, ♠ 6, ♠ Q, ♥ Q, ♣ K, ♣ 10, ♠ J, ♦ J. It is not usual to be *calling* so many cards with your original hand. Often you will be dealt only one or two combinations.

How do you get any of the cards that you are calling? That is where the play comes in. At each turn, you will

3

have the option of picking up the top card of the *discard pile*, which builds up on the starter, or of drawing blind the top card of the stock. That gives you eleven cards, so you then discard one card face up on the starter. Your hand will thus change character in accordance with what you draw and what you discard.

As non-dealer, it is your first turn. Will you take the ♦ 10 or will you draw from the stock? Had you been dealt the ♦ 10, you might keep it, together with the ♦ Q, on the chance of getting the ♦ J. But there is no sense in picking up the ♦ 10 to make this combination. You already have more combinations than you need — one will have to be broken up the moment you complete a second set. Furthermore, taking from the discard pile to make a mere combination is rarely good play — it is a desperate resort with a very poor hand. So you draw from the stock, getting the ♥ 10.

At this point—before discarding—you could meld the sixes; but you never have to meld until you want to. Once a set is melded, either player may *lay off* (add matching cards) on it; and it is advisable to hold a matched set as long as it seems safe to do so, to prevent the opponent from laying off. So you will keep the sixes, for the time being, and discard.

RUMMY

The ♥ 10 makes a combination with the ♥ J, therefore you may as well save it if you can find a useless card to discard. You do have one non-combined card, the ♠ K, so you discard it face up on the ♦ 10. A king is the least valuable card anyway, because it forms a sequence at only one end (K-Q-J) and costs 10 points if you are stuck with it, as you shall see.

Your opponent takes the ♠ K and then discards the ♥ Q. Yippee! you grab that card, and now you hold

It is unfortunate that you cannot use the ♥ Q twice over, to make three queens and to make a heart sequence, but a card may be used in one set only. What shall you discard? Certainly not a six; not the ♥ Q. That reduces the choice somewhat. Let's see how many *places* are left *open* in each case.

If you discard the ♣ J, you are calling: ♠ 9, ♠ 6, ♠ Q, ♥ 9 — four cards.

If you discard the ♦ Q, you are calling: ♠ 9, ♠ 6, ♣ K, ♣ 10 — four cards.

If you discard the ♣ Q, you are calling: ♠ 9, ♠ 6 — only two cards.

5

If you discard a spade, you are calling: ♠ Q, ♠ J, ♦ J, ♥ 9, ♣ K, ♣ 10 — six cards.

Evidently it is best to let go a spade. So you discard the ♠ 7. Your opponent picks up the ♠ 7 and discards the ♦ 9.

The presumption is that he holds either two more sevens or the ♠ 6-5. Keep that in mind, as his later play may show which is the case.

You draw from the stock and get the ♥ K. Now your hand is

What to discard? If you let go the ♠ 8, perhaps you will *feed* your opponent. But if you let go one of that beautiful mess of high cards, which shall it be? Probably, you meditate lugubriously, you will guess the wrong combination to break. Also, you would like to keep that heart sequence of four, because in this game you always have one odd card (left over from three sets of three) to match up with something.

You start to talk yourself into risking the discard of the ♠ 8. You argue "Surely the ♠ 6 is not in play yet — that would mean all four sixes were in the first half of the pack! He has three sevens, not a spade sequence." The argument sounds specious to your own ears, yet it holds a kernel of truth. To hold a spade sequence he must have two specific cards, the ♠ 6-5. To hold sevens, he needs two of three cards: ♥ 7, ♣ 7, ♦ 7. The abstract chances are better for the sevens.

You grit your teeth and lay down the ♠ 8. Your opponent draws from the stock, then says, "Guess I'll have to unload," and lays on the table

He discards the ♠ Q.

That card puts you *out*. You take it and lay down

The discard of the ♣ J leaves you with no more cards in your hand and ends the play. He has one card left, the ♦ J, counting 10 (see Scoring, page 9).

Since every deal is a separate game you collect your 10 points, then you deal the next hand, for the winner of each game deals next.

Laws of Rummy: *The draw.* Lower card has choice of seats and deals first. Ace ranks at all times below the deuce, the rank being K (high), Q, J, 10, 9, 8, 7, 6, 5, 4, 3, 2, A.

Dealing. Dealer gives each player ten cards, one at a time, beginning with his opponent. The remaining 32 cards are placed face down on the table to form the *stock*, and the top card is then turned up and laid beside the stock to form the *starter*.

Object of play is to get rid of all ten cards in the hand by forming them into *matched sets* of either of two types:

(a) Three or four of the same rank;

(b) Three or more in sequence in the same suit. Sequences end with the king (high) and ace (low).

The play. Non-dealer plays first. He may take the starter or the top card of the stock. After drawing, he must discard one card face up. Thereafter each player in turn may take the top card of the discard pile or the top of the stock, and must then discard one card. All discards are piled on the starter (if it was not taken) and must be kept squared up so that only the top card is identifiable.

A matched set of three or more cards may be *melded* (placed face up on the table) after the player has drawn but before he has discarded. Any number of sets may be melded at one turn. It is not compulsory to meld when able.

Cards that match may be added to any meld by either player. Example: If a player melds three kings, he or his opponent may later meld the fourth king. Example: A player melds ♥ 8-7-6; later the ♥ 5-4 may properly be melded in one turn. All such additional cards should be placed with the original sets, to avoid any possible ambiguity. Example: With three jacks and ♥ 10-9-8 already melded, the ♥ J must be clearly added to one or the other, at the owner's pleasure, to indicate whether the heart sequence is continued or closed.

A player *goes out* when he has melded exactly ten cards. He must make a discard at his last turn. Example: If a player has melded eight cards and is left with two aces, he may not meld three aces on drawing another ace, because he then has no card left to discard.

If no player has gone out by the time the stock is exhausted, the discard pile is shuffled and placed face down to form a new stock, the top card being turned up for a starter. Play continues until some player goes out, there being no drawn game.

Scoring. Play ends when either player goes out. This player is credited with all points left in the hand of his opponent, counting each face card 10, each ace 1, each other card its pip value. Each deal may be treated as a separate game, or the first to reach a total of 100 points may be declared the winner of a game.

Irregularities: *Misdeal.* The dealer must redeal, at his opponent's request, if he exposes an opponent's card in dealing.

A hand with incorrect number of cards is corrected by discarding without drawing, or by drawing without discarding, as the case may be. A player may not meld while his hand is incorrect. If a hand is short when the opponent goes out, every missing card counts 10 points.

Play out of turn must be recalled on the opponent's demand before the card illegally drawn is added to the offender's hand. Once the card is added to the hand, the play stands as a regular play in turn.

Exposed card. If a player illegally sees a card from the stock, he must show it to his opponent, who may either take it or cause it to be put in the center of the stock.

Incorrect meld. If a player has melded cards which are not a matched set, or has laid off cards which do not actually fit any meld on the table, he must restore those cards to his hand whenever attention is called to them. Any cards his opponent has laid off on such a set remain on the table.

Pointers on Play: It has been noted in the example game that it is rarely advisable to draw from the discard pile except to complete a set. The only exception is in the first one or two draws, when the original hand is singularly bereft of *combinations*. Suppose the original hand to be

If the starter is the ♦ 10, non-dealer might well take it, to make a double combination. The objection to such play is that it gives the opponent a clue to the contents of the hand. This objection has less weight when a high card is taken than a low card, for if the opponent is then careful not to discard "near" cards he undergoes the risk of holding a high-counting hand.

Modify the suits in the above hand to make a few more combinations, and it would be foolish to take the ♦ 10. For

example, look at the hand which follows this paragraph.
The near-sequences are just enough to tip the balance in
favor of drawing from the stock.

A point of importance in discarding is to avoid holding
two combinations that need the same card to fill. For example, after an early draw from the stock you hold

Some combination has to be broken up. The logical choice
is the ♦ 10-9. Should you draw the jack, you can use it
with the jacks. There is an "overlap" in the cards called for
by the jacks and the ♦ 10-9, but no overlap in the entire
hand if the ♦ 10-9 is abandoned. This point is noted also
in the example game, where the ♠ 8-7 was abandoned, in
part because of the three sixes. The simplest way to settle
these choices of discard, when a combination has to be

broken, is to count places open after each alternative discard.

The places open may be reduced by the fact that some of the cards called have previously been discarded, or that they are inferred to be held by the opponent as part of a set. The principal control you have on your own destiny is therefore to keep track of all the discards, and utilize all sources of inference as to your opponent's cards.

As a matter of course, when your opponent draws your discard, reckon that he has thereby completed or added to a set. Whether it is a set in rank or in sequence may be an open question: If so, keep it in mind and see what indication is given by his subsequent discards, or his later draws from the discard.

For example: As non-dealer, your hand is

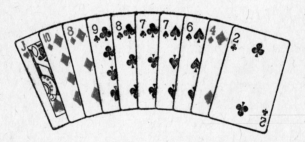

The starter is the ♠ 8. You take it, and elect to discard the ♥ J. Your opponent takes the ♥ J. You reckon that he now probably has three jacks or a heart sequence. Which? Nothing in your hand gives any indication. If he later discards any jack, or the ♥ Q or the ♥ 10, you will know for a certainty. But you need no such glaring tell-tale. If he discards the ♥ K or ♥ 9, there is good presumption that he has jacks rather than a sequence. If you draw any "near"

card — a jack, or a heart near the jack in rank — the chances become better that he has the kind of set that your card will not fit.

It is often possible to infer some holdings in the adverse hand from the ranks that your opponent *does not* draw from the discard pile, and from the ranks that he *does not* discard. Of course this source of inference develops only in the later stages of a game. Suppose that on about your eighth turn you draw a king from the stock, and this is the first king you have seen. The presumption is that your opponent is holding kings, so you are careful not to discard your king. The same caution must be observed as to any rank, when the first card of this rank you get comes to you late in the play.

Your first few discards have to be made with little or no knowledge of your opponent's hand. If you feed him at every turn, that's just too bad, but you are chargeable with no more than bad guessing. But as play continues there is less and less excuse for feeding him, because even if he fails to draw at all from the discard pile, keeping his hand a mystery, the discards themselves provide an increasing number of *safe* plays. To take an extreme example, if two sevens and the ♥ 8-6 have been discarded, you know that a discard of the ♥ 7 is perfectly safe — the card cannot possibly be used. Cards are more or less safe for discard according as more or less near cards have previously been discarded. When in doubt, discard a card of the same rank or in sequence with a card already in the discard pile, rather than launch into the unknown.

The question of whether or when to "unload" depends, of course, on your estimate of how near your opponent is to having a *rummy* hand (ten matched cards). In favor of unloading is that you reduce the amount by which you will be stuck if he goes out. Against unloading is that he can play on your melds, and that fact may enable him to go out. Generally speaking, you must think seriously of unloading after he has taken two cards from the discard pile. Also, think about unloading after three-fourths of the pack is in play, say after about eight draws.

Having inferred a set or a combination in the adverse hand, you naturally avoid feeding it. If you draw a matching card, you tuck it away with the resolve never to let it go. But what are you to do if you are stuck with several cards that fit your opponent's hand but not your own?

One possibility is to try to form sets of your own around these orphans. This is the necessary course when (on rare occasions) the stock becomes exhausted and the discard pile is made into a new stock. Such an outcome is scarcely possible unless both players hold like pairs or cards of the same suit alternating in sequence. Most of the time, however, one player goes out before the stock is exhausted. Not often is there time to re-form the hand to accommodate orphans.

If stuck with several orphans, you must usually unload your other melds as soon as possible. By doing so you may induce your opponent to "crack" also, and thus give you opportunity to play your orphans on his melds.

Being stuck with one orphan is not serious, since you may be able to discard it after forming your other cards into sets. But be wary of waiting for a *rummy* hand — one that can meld ten cards at once. The player who goes repeatedly for rummy, trying to catch his opponent with ten cards, loses on the average.

14

Rummy

If there is any one "secret" of winning at Rummy, it is to avoid the mannerisms through which the casual player proclaims the contents of his hand. On drawing from the stock a card that makes a combination or set, he inserts it in the middle of the fan and plucks his previously selected discard from the end. On completing a set, he abstracts the near cards held with the combination, now useless, and tucks them at one end of the fan, ready for discard. If he holds interlocking combinations and draws a matching card, he rearranges his hand in each possible way, to disclose the number of cards concerned. On seeing his opponent pick up a six from the discard pile, he moves his other six, of the pair that he commenced discarding *in toto,* from the discard end of the fan to the hold-till-hell-freezes-over end. On drawing a useless card from the stock, he does not put it in his hand but immediately drops it in the discard. If, in addition, he needs only one more card for rum, he closes his hand into a packet and draws from the stock with a portentous air.

The reader may say that it is not ethical to take advantage of such mannerisms on the part of an opponent. But with the best of intentions you cannot make yourself deaf, dumb and blind to the information thrust upon you by such an untutored innocent.

GIN RUMMY

Why You'll Like It: This is the most highly publicized game in the United States. Moving picture and radio stars are its rabid devotees. It isn't a new game—a Brooklynite, Whist-expert Elwood T. Baker, invented it in 1909 and named it "gin" because the parent game was called "rum" and he wanted the name of his variant to be similarly alcoholic—but it had a renascence in 1941 from which people haven't recovered yet. When Winston Churchill visited the U. S. in 1946 he temporarily dropped Bézique (see page 48) and took up Gin Rummy. Elwood T. Baker, incidentally, was a teetotaler who never tasted an intoxicating beverage in his life.

What You Need: A standard 52-card pack, with pencil and paper for keeping score.

Let's Play a Game: If you are not already familiar with Rummy, read the *Laws of Rummy*, page 8. Gin is the same as Rummy as to the general manner of play, the

objective of forming matched sets, and other principles.
The chief difference is that in Gin you do not need to meld
ten cards to go out—you may *knock* and end the play any
time the cards in your hand *not* matched in sets total 10
points or less—and the cards you're "stuck with" *don't*
count against you if they're matched in sets.

Now let's play. The pack is spread and you each draw a
card. His is the ♣ Q; yours, the ♦ 3. As his is higher, he
has choice of seats, and decides who shall deal first. He de-
crees that you shall deal. You shuffle the pack, he cuts, and
then you give ten cards to each hand, one at a time. You
put the rest of the pack face down to make the *stock*, and
turn the top card beside the stock. This starter is called the
upcard in Gin.

Your hand is

The upcard is the ♣ J. Your opponent says that he
doesn't want this card. Before he may draw from the stock,
he must give you the chance to take the upcard if you wish.
You refuse it also, and he draws. His discard is the ♠ Q.
You draw from the stock and get the ♥ 7. As this makes a
combination, you keep it and elect to discard the ♠ 10. He
picks up the ♠ 10 and discards the ♥ K. You make a men-
tal note that he probably has a set of three tens — not a
spade sequence, because he discarded the ♠ Q.

Your second draw is the ♥ 3. This does not fit with anything; nevertheless you keep it merely because it is a low card. You discard the ♦ K, although this gives up a combination. You are not trying to make three complete sets; you are trying to *reduce the count of your unmatched cards below 10*. Paste that in your hat and don't forget it.

Your opponent draws from the stock, then discards the ♦ 8. That you can use. You pick it up and let go the ♦ J. Your hand now is

On the next draw you get the ♥ A, which you keep, letting go the ♣ 9. Your opponent draws, then discards the ♠ 5, hitting you right in the middle! You grab the card, and now, after you discard the ♥ 7, you will have an unmatched count of only 10: 4 + 3 + 2 + A (1). That permits you to knock and end the play.

There is an alternative. You could play on, trying to get all ten of your cards matched, for a count of zero. Then you could "go gin" and earn a bonus of 20 points. But the chance of that is remote and meanwhile your opponent could go on improving his hand. It is usually wise to knock as soon as you can.

So you discard the ♥ 7 face down—the conventional way of showing that you knock—and spread your hand:

GIN RUMMY

Outside of the three eights and the spade sequence, you have just 10 points in unmatched cards, for the ace counts only 1 and therefore is the most valuable card in a Gin Rummy game. Your opponent's hand is

He lays off the ♠ 3-2 on your spade sequence, and his unmatched cards (the sixes and sevens and the ♦ 2) then total 28. You score 18 points, the difference between the counts. In your column on the score sheet you write 18, and draw a line under it. Now, being the winner, you will deal the next hand and play will continue until the game is won with a total score of 100.

Laws of Gin Rummy: *The draw*. Higher card has choice of seats and may deal first or require opponent to deal first. If cards of the same rank are drawn, they rank by suits: spades (high), hearts, diamonds, clubs.

Dealing. Dealer must give ten cards to each hand, one at a time, beginning with his opponent. The remaining 32 cards are placed face down to form the *stock*. The top card is turned over and placed beside it to form the *upcard*.

The play. Non-dealer may take the upcard. If he refuses it, dealer may take it. Thereafter each hand in turn may take the top of the discard pile or the top of the stock, and then discard one card. All discards are placed in one pile on the upcard (if it was not taken). The discard pile may be spread for examination of the discards.

Three or four cards of the same rank, and sequences of three or more cards of the same suit, are *matched sets*. Other cards in the hand are *unmatched*.

A player may knock if his unmatched cards, after he discards, will total 10 points or less. Prior to a knock, no cards of either hand should be exposed.

A knock ends the play, and both hands are then exposed. The knocker must arrange his sets in order, so that the intention is clear in any ambiguous case.

A hand of ten cards all matched in sets is called *gin*. The knocker should announce the fact, if he has a gin hand.

The opponent of the knocker is entitled to *lay off* any of his cards that fit with melds shown by the knocker (even if it is a gin hand). Cards so laid off count as matched cards.

If the fiftieth card of the pack is drawn and the player then discards, without knocking, the play ends as a draw, neither player scoring for the deal.

GIN RUMMY

Scoring. The unmatched cards left in each hand are totaled, counting each king, queen, jack or ten as 10, each ace as 1, each other card its pip value. If the knocker's total is less than his opponent's, the knocker wins the difference. If the knocker's total is equal to or greater than his opponent's, the latter scores the difference (if any) plus a bonus of 10 points for *undercut.* If the knocker has a gin hand, he scores a bonus of 20 points for *gin,* besides his opponent's count of unmatched cards; if the opponent is able to match all his cards (as by laying off), the knocker nevertheless receives the gin bonus and there is no other score.

Each deal (other than a draw through exhaustion of the stock) is construed a *box,* of which the player who scores is the winner. At the end of a game, each player is credited with 20 points for each box he has won.

The first player to reach 100 points wins a game. For so doing, he is credited with a *game bonus* of 100 points. An extra bonus of 100 points for *shutout* is credited the winner if the loser scored not a single point during the game. The box scores are entered, the totals won by each player are determined, and the higher wins by the difference of the totals.

Hollywood Gin is a method of scoring one game as though three were in progress at the same time. Separate double-columns are set up on the score sheet for Game 1, Game 2 and Game 3. The first score made by a player is entered only in Game 1; the second applies to Games 1 and 2; the third and all subsequent count in all three games. Separate box and game bonuses are awarded in each game. It may be agreed that the session will end when all three games have been completed. Or play may be continuous until terminated by later agreement—Game 4 is opened up as soon as any of the first three games is ended, and so on.

The illustration shows the beginning of a Hollywood Gin session. Jack's first score was 21, his second 10. Jill has won three times, making 14, 7 and 18. Observe the method of keeping the running total. Each new score is written below the previous total, the new total is written below, and then a horizontal line is drawn. The number of such lines shows the number of boxes won in each column.

GAME 1		GAME 2		GAME 3	
JACK	JILL	JACK	JILL	JACK	JILL
21	14	10	7		18
10	7		18		
31	21		25		
	18				
	39				

As soon as a player has scored 100 or more in any game, that game ends and scores made thereafter may be entered only in the unfinished games.

Irregularities: *Misdeal.* There must be a new deal if a card is exposed in dealing; or if a player has an incorrect number of cards and it is discovered before his first draw; or if it is discovered at any time that both hands are incorrect.

Incorrect number of cards. The player with the correct hand may either have a new deal or may require his opponent to correct his hand, by drawing without discarding or by discarding without drawing, as the case may be. After a knock, any card missing from a hand counts 10 points.

A card of the stock illegally seen must be placed face up beside the stock. The non-offender may take any such card at any turn until he draws from the stock; then the offender has the right to take any such card until he draws from the stock. After both players have drawn from the stock, all illegally exposed cards go among the discards.

Knocking illegally. If the knocker has a higher count than 10, his opponent may let the knock stand or require that play continue. If the opponent has exposed any of his cards before the discovery, he may require the knocker to continue play with all his cards exposed or he may permit play to continue as usual and cannot lose an undercut or gin bonus in that hand.

But if a knock is illegal only because the knocker has his cards incorrectly arranged, or has inadvertently discarded the wrong card, the knocker may correct the error.

An incorrect play (out of turn, or picking up the wrong discard) stands if correction is not demanded before the opponent draws.

Pointers on Play: If you are experienced in straight Rummy, as described on page 10, you must first of all learn that the strategy of Gin is markedly different.

In straight Rummy, you have to match up *ten* cards in order to go out. Most of the time, this can be done only by making three matched sets, then laying off the tenth card on one of them or on an adverse meld. Because that tenth card is often the sticker, you treasure as many different combinations as you can, and also count the possibility of increasing a set of three to four in reckoning *places open.* The chances of improvement are paramount in deciding what cards to keep and what to discard.

In Gin, you need only reduce your unmatched count to 10 or less to knock. Some of the time this is done by making only two matched sets. The *gin* hand is a rarity. The objective is therefore divided between making matched sets and collecting *low* unmatched cards. The advantage of keeping low cards often overrides the principle of discarding so as to keep the maximum chance of filling a set.

In straight Rummy, any cards left in your hand when your opponent goes out count against you, whether matched or not. You therefore have to give thought to *unloading*— melding your sets.

In Gin, there is no melding. You are stuck only with the count of the unmatched cards in your hand. Here you have to think of a different kind of *unloading* — the discard of combinations of high cards when you believe your opponent is near to knocking. In making the knock yourself, you have to reckon with a factor not present in *going out* at straight Rummy — after your knock, your opponent will be able to lay off on your melds, and he may thereby *undercut* you.

The value of low cards is such that, when the starter is an ace, the non-dealer usually will take it "blind," if only to keep the dealer from getting it. Some players will take a deuce or even a trey on the same principle. A card as low as a trey is rarely discarded early in the game. The early discards are almost invariably high cards — so much so that sometimes six to a dozen "tenth" cards are discarded consecutively before any lower card shows.

This fact suggests that it might be astute policy to keep face cards from the outset, counting on the opponent to *feed* the hand. Persuasive as is this notion, it has an inherent defect, which will be explained by the following example.

You pick up the hand shown on the opposite page, and your first draw is the ♣ 3. What shall you discard?

GIN RUMMY

It is true that you are more likely to fill the kings or the heart sequence than the diamond sequence or the fives. But

what if you do get a third king and the ♥ Q from your helpful opponent? With six cards in the two sets, you still have four cards. What are they to be? If you have saved either the diamond combination or the fives, you still have to fill a *third set* to knock. Now look at it the other way. Suppose you have saved the ♦ 4, ♣ 3, ♠ A. If you then fill any two sets, you can knock by drawing an ace or a deuce for your tenth card. This argument indicates that saving too many combinations, at the cost of letting go low cards, is equivalent to trying to fill three sets instead of two, manifestly a poor policy.

To save your three low cards, you will have to break up a combination. Why isn't it best to break up the diamond sequence or the fives, saving the combinations more likely to fill? As a matter of fact, a player could scarcely be criticized for embarking on this speculation. But it is inherently perilous. The play cannot be expected to be so simple as the exchange of the five-spots, say, for the ♥ Q and a king. There is a certain danger in the discard of middle and middling-low cards like the fives and the diamond sequence — the opponent is more likely to need them than the tenth cards. If this hand draws other dangerous cards, it may find itself feeding the opponent at every turn in order to save the kings and the heart sequence. Contrariwise, if this hand resolves to unload the tenth cards, it is assured of four reasonably safe discards whatever the draw. Above all, the discard of the tenth cards is not likely to become increasingly dangerous as the play progresses, as is true of the middle cards. If the opponent does not start with two kings or a high heart sequence, he is unlikely to save such combinations drawn later.

Having seen the case for ditching high-card combinations, let us look at the other side of the picture. Suppose that you pick up

To knock with only two matched sets, this hand will have to draw two cards to fill the sets, together with three other cards totaling less than six. The prospect here is actually better for *filling three sets* — requiring only three cards. It would be *folly* not to keep the highest seven cards for at least three draws. The normal expectation is that the opponent will commence by unloading his unmatched tenth cards. Only if he fails to feed you within three draws (make it five or six if you are not a 'fraid-cat) should you begin to think of unloading.

GIN RUMMY

Few games end with a gin hand. Failure to knock, when you need one card to make gin, is a frivolity properly reserved to a game that has almost exhausted the stock and where you know that there is some risk your opponent will undercut you if you knock. Gin Rummy is a fast-moving, fast-scoring game; the expert aims to knock at the first possible opportunity. The knocker, if he has not dallied a moment, wins four out of five times. This batting average can be improved by watching for the signs that your opponent will undercut you if you knock.

The undercut almost invariably results from laying off. Here is a feature different from straight Rummy. If you draw a king, and know that your opponent has the other three kings, in straight Rummy you are stuck. To go out, you must manage to build your king into a sequence, or induce him to meld so that you can lay off. But in Gin your king is in effect a matched card, provided that he knocks, not you. You are stuck in another way: the king will never count against you, but may stand in the way of your knocking. So you string along as best you can, collecting what you can to undercut him.

This policy is sometimes detectable from the discards. Suppose you know that your opponent has two sets (inferred from his drawing of two cards from the discard pile). The game is well advanced, and he discards a very low card. Why did he not save it for knocking, or why has he failed to knock? The presumption is that he has one or two cards matching your sets and *cannot* knock. This is the time to be wary of knocking, yourself, without a very low count.

27

PINOCHLE

Why You'll Like It: One of the most popular of all
two-hand games played in the United States, Pinochle dates
from the 1860's and was the first game of a family which
now contains some of our most popular games for three
and four players.

What You Need: The Pinochle deck of 48 cards: twelve
cards in each suit, comprising two aces (highest-ranking),
two tens, two kings, two queens, two jacks, and two nines
(lowest-ranking). Don't overlook that the cards rank in
the central European fashion—the ten below the ace and
above the king.

Some score with chips or with special markers, but pencil
and paper will do.

Let's Play a Game: You and your opponent draw a
card each from the shuffled pack. His card proves to be a
king; yours is a ten. Having the higher card, you deal first.

PINOCHLE

You pick up the 48 cards, shuffle them, and let your opponent cut them. Then you deal two hands of 12 cards each, in batches of three cards at a time. You turn over the next card of the pack — the 25th — and slip it partly under the remaining packet of 23 cards, which stays in the middle of the table and forms the *stock*. This turned card fixes the trump suit for this deal. It happens to be the ♥ Q; therefore hearts will be trumps.

Pick up your hand and sort the cards into suits and rank, thus:

Before we commence play, let's find out what we are trying to do.

The Melds. Whenever you win a trick, you are entitled to meld—place face up on the table—any combination of cards in your hand that is listed below, and so score the number of points shown.

"Flush" (A-10-K-Q-J of the trump suit)	150
"Hundred aces" (one ace of each suit)	100
"Eighty kings" (one king of each suit)	80
"Sixty queens" (one queen of each suit)	60
"Forty jacks" (one jack of each suit)	40
"Forty Pinochle" (one queen of spades and one jack of diamonds)	40

Trump marriage (one king and one queen of
  trumps)   40

Common marriage (one king and one queen
  of a plain suit)   20

Dix (one nine of trumps—pronounced deece)   10

There are various rules covering melding, which, later
on, you may consult (page 39).

The Card Values. After the play is finished, you will run
through the cards you have taken, and score for each as
follows:

Each ace	11
Each ten	10
Each king	4
Each queen	3
Each jack	2
Each nine	0
For winning last trick	10

On With the Game: Since you dealt, your opponent
leads first. His lead is the ♠ 10.

You may play any card in your hand — you do not have
to follow suit (yet). You can take the ♠ 10 with the ♠ A,

or you can trump it with any heart. Do you want the trick? Reasons for taking a trick are (a) you want to meld; (b) you want to collect high cards, especially aces and tens. First look to see if you have anything to meld. You have indeed— a common marriage in spades and the dix. What will it cost you to win the trick? Don't forget to ask yourself that! If you give up the ♠ A, you have ruined your chance of making 100 aces by drawing the ♦ A. If you trump, you give up a good start on a flush. Even trumping with the ♥ 9 is out of the question, for you need it to get the ♥ Q (as is explained later). Besides, you can't score 10 for the dix by playing it in a trick — you have to meld it first.

Better be patient and let him have the trick, discarding your useless ♦ 9.

Having won the trick, your opponent takes the opportunity to make a meld, putting the ♥ K Q face up on the table. He announces "Forty" and you — who were elected to keep score — write that amount in his column of the scoresheet. Your opponent draws the top card of the stock, and you draw the next. After each trick you will each restore your hand to 12 cards by drawing from the stock, the winner of the trick first.

Your draw is the ♠ 9, so your hand now is:

Your opponent, having won the previous trick, leads to the next. His lead is the other ♠ 9. Again you decide not to win it at the cost of breaking up a possible meld, so you play your ♠ 9. He takes the trick — when two identical cards are played, the leader wins the trick. This time your opponent draws from the stock at once, without melding. Your second draw is the ♠ 10, and your hand now is:

Your opponent leads the ♠ J. It almost seems as though he is wise to the fact that spade leads have been embarrassing to you! But now you are ready for him. The ♠ 10 cannot be used in a meld, but is handy for taking his ♠ J. You hasten to show the ♥ 9, which you are entitled to exchange for the ♥ Q, the turned card under the pack. You want that queen, for then you lack only the king for a flush. You slide out the ♥ Q from under the stock and add it to your hand; you take the ♥ 9 from your hand and slide it under the stock, where it will remain till the stock is all drawn. You announce and score "Ten" for the meld of the dix.

You can't meld the marriage in spades at this time, because you may make only one meld at a time. It was important to count the dix first, so as to get the trump queen.

Your draw from the stock is the ♣ J, and your hand now is as shown at the top of the next page.

As you won the last trick, it is now your lead. It is easy to pick the card, since you hold just one which can never be part of a meld — the ♦ 10. Your opponent discards the ♣ 9, so you gather the trick, then meld and score "Twenty" for the spade marriage. You draw the ♦ 9, and have:

On the table:

In your hand:

Your lead of the ♦ 9 brings out the ♦ A from your opponent — and he then melds 100 aces. Since you can never get a ♦ A, your own hope of 100 aces goes glimmer-

ing. But business picks up when your next draw proves to
be the ♥ K. Look at your hand now!

On the table:

In your hand:

Your opponent leads the ♠ J. You want to win the trick;
what shall you play? You might put on either the ♠ K or
♠ Q from the table — you may play cards from your melds
just as from your hand. But you surely don't want to let go
the ♠ K! The three kings in your hand can be added to it
to make eighty kings. The ♠ Q could be used in a meld of
pinochle, should you draw the ♦ J. The ♠ A alone cannot
be used in any meld, so win the lead of the ♠ J with it.

You can make only one meld at this turn. Which shall it
be? If you meld the flush at once, you score 150 but lose the
score for the marriage. By melding the marriage on this
turn, then the ♥ A-10-J on a later turn, you can score 190
for the same five cards. The only question is, will you have
time to make three separate melds? There are twelve cards
left in the stock—six turns. You decide to play for the
works, so you meld the trump marriage.

PINOCHLE

Your draw is the ♣ 9, and your cards are now

On the table:

In your hand:

You lead the ♣ A and your opponent plays the ♣ J. You lay down the ♥ A-10-J, completing the flush for 150. Your draw is the ♦ K, and your cards are now

On the table:

In your hand:

35

At the moment, your total score is 220, and your opponent has 140. The only chance he has of winning is to meld the other flush. You can avert this possibility by leading trumps, because he cannot win a trump trick and still have the cards left for a flush. So you now lead the ♥ J. Your opponent discards the ♣ Q. You place the ♣ K and a ♦ K on the table, announcing "Eighty" for the kings.

In the ensuing play, your opponent captures your lead of the ♥ 10 with the ♥ A and melds the other dix. He wins the last trick. Under the rules he must show you his last draw; it is the ♣ Q. Your last draw is the dix which previously you exchanged for the trump queen.

Now each of you picks up his melds and adds them to his hand. If you remember all the cards that have been played, you will know that your opponent holds

Your last twelve cards are

PINOCHLE

Your opponent won the preceding trick, so he leads — the ♥ 9. *You must play the* ♥ *A*. In the play of these last twelve cards, you must follow suit if you can; you must win a trump lead if you can; and you must play a trump if you cannot follow to the lead of another suit.

Having won the ♥ A, you lead the ♠ Q. Your opponent wins it, leads his ♥ 10 to catch your nine, takes his ♦ A and ♦ 10, and leads the ♦ J.

You win the ♦ K and lead your last diamond, which he trumps. Now he leads the ♣ Q. He is going to lose his tricks early, to make sure of scoring 10 for "last."

You could win the ♣ Q with a king, but instead you play the ♣ 10. It is the only trick you can win, and you want to take in the card worth 10 points instead of a king, worth only 4 points. Your opponent gets the remaining tricks.

You each count your cards: He has 155, including last; you have only 95. (The combined count of cards, including last, is always 250. If some other total is reached, a recount is required.) But you had 300 in melds, so you have 395 (which counts as 400), while your opponent melded only 150 and has a total score of 305.

If you are playing that each deal is a game, you have won this game. But the usual style is to play for 1,000 points, in which case the game continues and your opponent is the next dealer.

Don't imagine that there is as much melding in every deal as there was in the foregoing example. You were doubly lucky — you drew good cards, and perhaps your opponent, by shrewder play, could have prevented you from getting in all your melds.

Laws of Pinochle: *The Deal.* The player who cuts the higher card deals the first hand. Thereafter the deal alternates. (In some localities the winner of the previous hand deals the next). After the deck has been shuffled and cut, the dealer gives twelve cards to each player, either three or four cards at a time, beginning with his opponent. The 25th card is then turned face up on the table; and the suit of that card (called the *trump card*) is the trump suit during that hand.

Early Play. The non-dealer leads to the first trick; but thereafter the winner of a trick leads to the next trick. When leading, a player may lead any card from his hand.

During the play of the first twelve tricks, the *early play*, the opponent of the leader may play any card from his hand. During the play of the last twelve tricks, the *final play*, the opponent of the leader must follow suit if he can; play a trump if he cannot follow suit; and, when a trump is led, must win the trick if he can. If unable to so play, he may play any card.

(In the foregoing, the term "hand" includes all of the twelve cards belonging to the player, whether actually held in the hand or melded on the table.)

A trick which contains one trump is won by the trump; any other trick is won by the higher card of the suit led. If both cards are identical, the leader wins the trick.

The Stock. The winner of a trick draws the top card of the stock to restore his hand to twelve cards. The loser of the trick draws the next card from the stock. When both hands have been restored to twelve cards, the winner of the previous trick may lead to the new trick. The trump card is considered the last card of the stock (although it was originally the top card of the stock). The player who draws the next-to-last card of the stock must show it to his opponent before adding it to his hand.

Melding. A player may make a meld directly after he has won a trick provided he has not yet drawn from the stock. The loser of a trick may not meld; the winner of a trick may meld only before drawing from the stock; and all melding ceases once the stock has been exhausted.

A player makes his meld by putting the cards of the meld face up on his side of the table. It is customary for the melder to announce the amount (in points) of his meld as he puts the card or cards down. Cards used in a meld are available to be led or played but may not be put back into the hand during the early play. When the stock is exhausted, any melded cards which may still be on the table are picked up; and each player then begins the late play with a full complement of twelve cards held in his hand.

If the trump card is a dix, the dealer scores 10 points at once without having to win a trick. When the trump card is anything other than a dix, the winner of a trick may take a dix from his hand (before drawing from the stock) and substitute it for the trump card, at the same time scoring 10 points.

The holder of the other dix may (after winning a trick and before drawing from the stock) substitute it for the first dix, scoring 10 points as he does so. (In practice, the substitution of one dix for another is not made; the holder of the second dix simply shows it.) In some circles, the holder of the second dix may show it and score 10 points at any time, if he has theretofore won any trick — even though he did not win the preceding trick.

The melds other than the dix are:

CLASS A

Flush (A-10-K-Q-J of the trump suit) 150
Trump marriage (one king and one queen of trumps) 40
Common marriage (one king and one queen of a plain suit) 20
Dix (one nine of trumps) 10

CLASS B

Hundred aces (one ace of each suit) 100
Eighty kings (one king of each suit) 80
Sixty queens (one queen of each suit) 60
Forty jacks (one jack of each suit) 40

CLASS C

Pinochle (one queen of spades and one jack of diamonds) 40

A card once melded may not be used as part of another meld in the same class, e. g., if pinochle is melded, a second meld of pinochle by the same player requires both the other ♦ J and the other ♠ Q.

A card once melded may be used as part of another meld of a different class, with the provisos that:

(a) For each new meld the player must use at least one additional card from his hand;

(b) If a flush is melded, the K-Q do not score in addition as a trump marriage, and neither card may be used as part of a subsequent trump marriage. But if a trump marriage is melded first, a flush may be scored by adding the A-10-J of trumps at a later turn.

Final Play. The player who draws the last face-down card of the stock must show it to his opponent, who then draws the exposed trump card or dix. There is no more melding. The last twelve tricks are played, with the following differences in rules: A player must follow suit to the card led, if he can; if a trump is led, he must win the trick if he can; if he cannot follow suit, but has a trump, he must play a trump.

When the last trick has been played, each player scores as follows for cards won in tricks:

Each ace	11	Each queen	3
Each ten	10	Each jack	2
Each king	4	Winning last trick	10

Scoring. Two methods of scoring are widely used in two-hand Pinochle:

1. Each hand a unit by itself; and
2. Game is 1,000 points.

Whichever method of scoring is used, the winner of the game is customarily credited merely with one point for game, regardless of the margin by which he wins.

Declaring Out. When game is 1,000 points, the game may be won by totalling the score at the end of some deal in which one player's score has gone over 1,000 points. However, either player may "declare out" during the course of a deal. Play then stops immediately, and the declaring player counts his points. If his total is then 1,000 points or more, he wins the game. Otherwise, his opponent wins the game; and the opponent's score is reckoned as 1,000 (unless it is actually greater).

If no one declares out and both players reach 1,000 on the same deal, play continues as though game originally had been 1,250; and thus, "game" may become 1,500 or even more.

Irregularities: *Dealing.* If the cards are dealt in any manner but either three at a time or four at a time, the non-dealer may demand a new deal. Likewise the non-dealer may demand a new deal if any of his own cards or any of the cards in the stock are exposed (but not if dealer's cards are exposed) ; or if either player is dealt fewer than twelve cards.

Non-dealer may, instead, either condone the irregularity or require that it be corrected (e.g., by turning over an exposed card, or by dealing additional cards until each player has twelve.)

There *must* be a new deal if either player receives too many cards; and either player may call attention to this before each has played to the first trick. Any irregularity in the deal stands as regular after both players have played to the first trick.

Drawing. If a card is found faced in the stock, it is turned face down and left in the same position in the stock.

If the winner of a trick draws two cards from the stock, seeing his opponent's card, he must show his own card.

If the loser of a trick improperly draws first, the winner may require correction and may look at the loser's draw. If both players draw incorrectly, the draw stands regularized.

If the loser of a trick draws his own card and the card beneath it, he must take his correct card; and his adversary may look at both cards of the following draw and may choose either for himself at the end of the next trick. If he selects the card which the offender has not seen, he need not show it.

In all of these cases, to *draw* means to take a card from the stock and look at it.

Irregular hand. If one player forgets to draw and plays to the next trick, he must draw two cards the next time.

42

PINOCHLE

If both players forget to draw, each must draw two cards the next time.

If either player is found to have too many cards during the play, he omits drawing until his count is correct; and similarly if *both* players hold too many cards.

A player who holds too many or too few cards may not meld until he has first corrected his count and then won a trick.

Melding. A meld is void, and the cards which comprise it must be picked up, if it is put down after a card has been drawn from the stock or if it is made by the loser of a trick.

If a player attempts to make more than one meld at an otherwise proper occasion, he must make one of the melds announced and must pick up any cards not used for that purpose.

If a player tries to make an impossible meld, his attempt is cancelled, and he may pick up without penalty the cards put down in error. (In all of the foregoing cases the penalty is either slight or non-existent because the offender gains nothing, while giving his opponent information about his hand.)

An incorrect meld stands as regular if it is not corrected before both players have played to the next trick.

Play. If a player leads out of turn, he may be required to take his card back; but if a card is played to such a lead, it stands as regular.

If a player drops one or more cards from his hand; or if he attempts to play more than one card to a trick, he may choose the card he intends to play and pick up the cards dropped or played in error.

A card is played when it is withdrawn from the hand (or from a meld on the table) with apparent intent to play and placed near the middle of the playing surface so that the opponent can see the face of the card (even though the player's hand is not removed from the card). Once a card is played it may not be withdrawn.

Either player may look back at the last trick before playing to the current trick. If a player looks back beyond the last trick, the value of his tricks in that deal is cancelled. (This may mean the loss of the game if the player has declared out and needs his trick score to total 1,000 points.)

Revoke. A revoke may occur only during the last twelve tricks, and consists of a failure (a) to follow suit when able; or (b) to ruff, holding trumps but no card of the suit led; or (c) to play a higher trump (when able) on a trump lead.

If a card is found on the floor in such position that it *might* have been dealt to or held by a player, the player whose hand is deficient is deemed to have held it in his hand during the play; and he is liable for any revoke caused by failure to play it.

The revoking player loses the revoke trick and all cards in both hands at the time the revoke occurs.

Incorrect pack. If the pack is found to contain either too many or too few cards (except when a missing card is found on the floor, as cited in the paragraph above), the current deal is void. All previous deals, however, stand as regular.

Incorrect stock. If there are three cards left in the stock at the end of the early play, and each player has twelve cards, the trump card is not drawn and is not counted in the count of cards; neither player need show the last card he draws.

Scoring. Any error in scoring may be corrected until both players have played to the first trick of the next deal, after which the score stands as regular.

Pointers on Play: In most deals, skilful play of the cards (as distinguished from melding) may produce about 30 or 40 points more than unskilful play of the same cards. Most of the melds come to far more than this, and it is therefore clear that melding is more important than the play of the cards.

Good players try to avoid leading or playing cards which will be needed later on for a meld. This applies also to cards which *may* be needed later on. A player who holds three kings in different suits will avoid playing any of them, since he has a fairly good chance of drawing the fourth and melding 80 points. Once a card has been melded, however, it is available for play (unless it is needed as part of a later meld). Hence it is usually sound policy to make melds at the first opportunity—not only for fear that a later opportunity will not be offered, but also in order to free cards for leading or playing.

Tens are ideal cards with which to win tricks. Their point value is very high and they are useless for melding. They are also excellent cards to lead, since the opponent will be reluctant to win with either an ace or a trump for fear of spoiling his chance to meld 100 aces or a trump flush. It is not safe to lead a ten when your opponent has already melded 100 aces, however, since then his aces are available for play; nor when your opponent has abandoned hope of melding 100 aces.

A player who has both aces of a suit, or other duplicate cards, can usually afford to spare one to win a trick. However, the play of a duplicate card often reveals to the opponent that he cannot hope to draw some particular meld; and this releases for play cards that he would otherwise hold in his hand hopefully. Good players, therefore, usually conceal duplicates as long as possible.

When one card has been melded and the duplicate is held in the hand, the card on the table should be played rather than its duplicate from the hand.

To a large extent it is every player's style to save cards for possible melds. When, however, a hand is practically worthless in melds, it is sound play to win a trick whenever possible. The points thus won may help to compensate for the lack of melds; and the winning of the tricks may prevent your opponent from melding his maximum amount. Sometimes, moreover, your opponent may abandon melding possibilities because your play has led him to believe that you hold duplicates of some card played to win a trick. Thus, you may play an ace simply to win a trick in a desperate hand; but he may conclude that you have the duplicate ace and play some aces of his own, destroying his own chance of melding 100 aces.

This style of wide-open play will seldom win a deal. Since two or three fortunate draws may improve an apparently hopeless hand, wide-open play should be postponed for at least three tricks.

When trying to prevent your opponent from winning a trick during the early part of the melding period, the soundest policy is to keep leading cards from a single suit—preferably your longest non-trump suit.

46

PINOCHLE

Toward the beginning of the melding period it usually pays to let your opponent win a trick when you have no meld of your own. Toward the middle of the melding period, it pays to win a trick even with no meld in your hand if you have some long side suit to lead and can reasonably expect that your opponent will have difficulty in winning a trick in that suit. Toward the end of the melding period, it usually pays to win a trick when you can.

When only two cards are left in the stock and no melds are feared, it is a nice point whether to win the twelfth trick for its point value or to lose it and draw the exposed trump to add to your trump length in the final play. Care must be taken, however, not to leave an unguarded ace in the hand which loses the twelfth trick, if the opponent has the other ace of that suit.

Memory is a vital factor in skilful play during the final period, since the good player invariably knows the exact cards in his opponent's hand.

The struggle for the last trick is usually a battle of trumps. There are two ways to exhaust your opponent's trumps:

1. Leading trumps yourself; and
2. Leading another suit to force him to trump.

Of these, the second method is by far the more common. In rare hands, you may hold a non-trump suit containing several high cards. To prevent your opponent from trumping these high side cards, you may wisely draw trumps. This may cost you the last trick, but may be worth the loss.

SIX-PACK BÉZIQUE

Why You'll Like It: You'll read of Six-pack Bézique (or "Chinese" Bézique) in stories about the who's who of the Riviera-Newport-Biarritz set. It's a fast, exciting, high-scoring game—as it has to be, to capture the fancy of jaded, blasé international cafe society.

Originally a French game (the name is pronounced bay-ZEEK) Bézique is played in many different forms — the most popular American variant is Pinochle (page 28). If you have played Pinochle, you'll find Bézique easy to learn. If you haven't, some of the rules may seem strange to you at first, but the later enjoyment of the game will reward the effort of learning it.

What You Need: Take six packs of cards and remove all cards below the seven, leaving thirty-two cards in each pack—A, 10, K, Q, J, 9, 8, 7 of each suit. The cards rank in that order, a ten winning from anything but an ace.

You'll also need poker chips, if you don't have a special Bézique scoring device. Scoring is too rapid and too high for pencil and paper. Put all the chips in a pile at the side of the table, letting each blue chip count 1,000 points, each red chip 100 and each white chip 10. As you score, you will take the proper number of chips from the pile.

Let's Play a Game: You and your opponent both shuffle the cards, trading portions back and forth so that the entire pack—there are 192 cards altogether—will be thoroughly mixed.

Now you each cut a card. You get a ten and your opponent a queen; stick these cards back in the pack. Low deals first, so your opponent is the first dealer. He lifts off a portion of the pack and without touching this portion you try to guess how many cards he took. If he took exactly twenty-four cards, he will score 250; if you guessed right, you will score 150.

Your opponent deals, one card at a time face down, until you have twelve cards each. The undealt cards are toppled over at the side of the table, between you, to be the *stock*. You pick up your hand:

You can't appraise your hand, of course, without knowing the principal object of play, which is to score for *declarations* (Pinochle players would call them "melds"). Here are the combinations that count:

TABLE OF DECLARATIONS

Sequence (A-K-Q-J-10): In trumps, 250; in any other suit, 150.

Marriage: K-Q of trumps, 40; K-Q of any other suit, 20.

Four of a kind in trumps: Four aces, 1,000; four tens, 900; four kings, 800; four queens, 600; four jacks, 400.

Four of a kind in any suits (they do not have to include one of each suit): Four aces, 100; four kings, 80; four queens, 60; four jacks, 40. Four tens do not count.

Bezique: This is by far the most important declaration, and will have the greatest influence on your play. A bezique is always the queen of the trump suit and a specified jack of opposite color:

If spades are trumps, ♠ Q and ◇ J.
If diamonds are trumps, ◇ Q and ♠ J.
If hearts are trumps, ♡ Q and ♣ J.
If clubs are trumps, ♣ Q and ♡ J.

Bezique counts only 40; but *double bezique* (two each of the proper queens and jacks) count 500; *triple bezique*, 1,500; *quadruple bezique*, 4,500.

You must know the declarations to play; until you have learned them by heart, write them out on a card and keep it beside you.

At the start there is no trump suit. The first marriage (or sequence) to be declared will establish the trump.

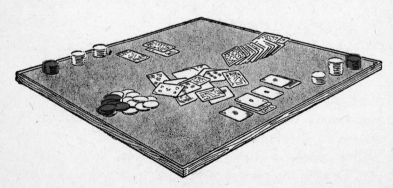

Six-Pack Bezique

Now take another look at your hand:

Your opponent dealt; that makes it your first lead. You may lead any card; but what? Until you know what suit will be trumps, you should hold on to all cards which might figure in the higher-scoring declarations. Especially you must keep *all queens and jacks*. You have no marriage with which to make the trump, and must be prepared for any. So you lead a worthless card — the seven of diamonds.

Your opponent plays the seven of spades. *It is not necessary to follow suit.* You win the trick because he did not play a higher card of the suit you led. Once there is a trump suit, a trump will also win from any lead of another suit.

The cards of the first trick remain face up on the table; the cards in the tricks do not count for anyone, so throughout the game they will remain in a loose pile in the center of the table.

But there is one advantage to the winning of tricks: Only after you win a trick may you declare and score one of the counting combinations. Usually, when you have nothing to declare you do not particularly care who wins the trick.

Now having won the trick and having no declaration, you draw the top card of the stock to restore your hand to twelve cards. Your opponent draws the next card. You drew a jack of clubs, and your hand is:

Having won the previous trick, you lead again. Still protecting your possible scoring cards, you lead the ♣ 9. This is a better lead than the seven, because to win it your opponent must play some possible scoring card. If the nine wins, you can declare your four jacks and score 40.

The ♣ 9 does win, and before drawing you put the four jacks face up on the table in front of you and take four white chips from the pile on the table. You draw — the ♥ K. Your opponent draws. Now you have

On the table:

In your hand:

Six-Pack Bezique

The cards declared remain on the table, but you may lead or play them as though they were in your hand. However, you want to keep the jacks for possible future béziques. You lead the ♣ 7.

Your opponent wins this trick with the ♣ 10 and declares the K-Q of hearts, scoring 40. Now hearts are trumps. The ♥ Q and ♣ J become the two most important cards in the pack. Other queens and jacks become of minor importance.

Your opponent, having won the trick, draws; you draw and get the ♦ K. Now you have:

On the table:

In your hand:

The lead is the ♣ 8. You put on your ten and win the trick. The ten is no longer likely to figure in a declaration, and you want this trick because you proceed to score 150 by adding the A, 10, K, Q of diamonds to the jack on the table. This gives you a non-trump sequence, known in the slang of the game as a "back door." Of course, you could have put down the ♦ K-Q first, scoring 20, and later added the ♦ A-10 for the 150 points; and now that you have declared the entire sequence, you may no longer declare the marriage. But in a high-scoring game like Six-pack Bézique, 20 points are not worth wasting time on.

You draw another ace of hearts; your opponent draws. Your hand now is:

On the table:

In your hand:

You promptly lead the queen of diamonds from the table. This is an important feature of the game: Getting rid of that queen will permit you, the next time you win a trick, to put down the other queen of diamonds from your hand and score 150 points all over again. You may not do this while the full scoring combination is on the table, so you break it up.

Your opponent wins your queen of diamonds and adds a jack of clubs to the queen of hearts he declared before; he scores 40 for bézique. He will not break up this combination; bézique is the one declaration that you do not break up, for to add a second bézique will score 500 more, provided the first bézique is still on the table; adding a third will score 1,500 more, provided the first two are still on the

SIX-PACK BEZIQUE

table, and so on. If a player is fortunate enough to get quadruple bézique, for a 4,500-point score, then he will break it up, for restoring it with one of the bézique cards will count an extra 4,500 each time.

You are permitted to declare two or more combinations at once, but only one may be scored at a time. Thus, if you have ♥ K (trumps) and ♣ J already on the table, after winning a trick you may put down the ♥ Q and announce, "Forty for bézique and forty to score," the extra 40 being for the marriage in trumps. The next time you win a trick, you score the other 40. You may have any number of pending declarations at the same time, and after winning a trick you may choose which one to score.

Now your game is well under way, and in this manner play proceeds. When only ten or twelve cards remain in the stock, there is a mad scramble to win tricks and declare all available combinations, and to keep the opponent from making any declarations, for after the last two cards of the stock have been drawn there is no more declaring.

However, you try not to weaken your hand too much in this closing period, for there is a play-off which is important: Having drawn the last cards of the stock, you and your opponent pick up any cards you have exposed on the table, so that you each have twelve cards. The player who won the previous trick leads. The object now is to win the last trick.

In this play-off, the rules change radically. You must follow suit to the lead if you can. *You must win the trick if you can*, by trumping if you cannot follow suit. The player who wins the last trick scores 250.

Having finished this play, you compare the total scores.

The player with the higher score is the winner and adds 1,000 to his score; if you have scored 4,320 and your opponent has 3,690, you win 4,300 + 1,000, less 3,600, a difference of 1,700 points in your favor. Anything less than 100 is disregarded, unless the winning of a close game depends on it.

There is also the feature of the *rubicon*; if the loser has scored less than 3,000 points, the winner gets *all* the points that were scored by both players. This has a profound effect on the strategy of play. In the late stages of the game, when a player sees that he is virtually sure to be rubiconed, he tries to score as little as possible so as not to add to the winner's score.

The following rules give in detail the procedure of play and scoring.

Laws of Six-pack Bezique: *Cards.* Six 32-card packs, A, 10, K, Q, J, 8, 7 of each suit, shuffled together. The packs may differ in back design and color, but not in size.

Rank of cards. A (high), 10, K, Q, J, 9, 8, 7.

Preliminaries. Both players shuffle. Each player lifts a packet and shows the bottom card; high has choice of seats and whether or not to deal. (Since the deal is a disadvantage, he invariably chooses not to deal.) In case of a tie in cutting, the players cut again.

The deal. Dealer lifts off a portion of the pack. Without touching them, non-dealer states his estimate of the number of cards so lifted off. Dealer gives one card at a time, face down, to his opponent and then to himself, until each has twelve cards. If dealer lifted off exactly 24 cards, he scores 250. If non-dealer estimated correctly, he scores 150.

Six-Pack Bezique

All undealt cards are placed at the side of the table as the *stock*.

Object of the game. To score points with *declarations* and by winning the last trick.

Play of the cards. Non-dealer leads first; he may lead any card. Dealer may play any card to it (until the stock is exhausted, it is not necessary to follow suit). The card led loses the trick to a higher card of the same suit (or a trump, if any other suit is led), but wins the trick from any other card.

No points are scored for cards won in tricks. The tricks are left face up, where they fall.

The winner of the trick, after *declaring* if he wishes to (see below), draws the top card of the stock to restore his hand to twelve cards; then his opponent draws similarly.

The winner of each trick leads to the next.

Declarations. After winning a trick and before drawing, a player may declare and score any of the following combinations:

Sequence (A-K-Q-J-10): In trumps, 250; in any other suit, 150.

Marriage: K-Q of trumps, 40; K-Q of any other suit, 20.

Four of a kind in trumps: Four aces, 1,000; four tens, 900; four kings, 800; four queens, 600; four jacks, 400.

Four of a kind in any suits (they do not have to include one of each suit): Four aces, 100; four kings, 80; four queens, 60; four jacks, 40. Four tens do not count.

Bézique: If spades are trumps, ♠ Q and ♦ J.

If diamonds are trumps, ♦ Q and ♠ J.

If hearts are trumps, ♥ Q and ♣ J.

If clubs are trumps, ♣ Q and ♥ J.

Bézique counts 40; *double bézique* (two each of the proper queens and jacks), 500; *triple bézique,* 1,500; quadruple *bézique,* 4,500.

A declaration is made by placing the required cards face up on the table and leaving them there until they are played to tricks. Any declared card may be played to a trick as though it were part of the player's hand.

The trump suit. The suit of the first marriage declared becomes trump. If a sequence is declared before a marriage, the suit of the sequence becomes trump.

The same suit may not be trump in two consecutive deals. A marriage in the trump suit of the previous deal may be declared before the new trump is established, counting 20.

Rules of declaring. Only one declaration may be scored in a turn, but more than one declaration may be announced. For example, hearts are trumps and a player has ♥ K on the table; upon winning a trick he puts down ♥ Q and ♣ J, scores 40 for bézique and announces 40 still to score for the royal marriage. He may score the additional 40 the next time he wins a trick, provided all the cards essential to the declaration are still on the table at that time. A player may have several unscored declarations pending at the same time, and may select the order in which he will score them. He is never required to score a declaration, whether or not he previously announced it.

A player who has a declaration still unscored must announce it at every trick, whether or not he wins the trick.

When a card has been played from a declaration on the table, and that declaration is then restored by the addition of an appropriate card, the full value of the declaration is scored again. This may be repeated any number of times. For example, a player has scored 100 for four aces. He plays one of the aces. The next time he wins a trick, he may add an ace and score 100 again. However, so long as the four aces are on the table, a player may not score 100 by adding the fifth ace.

A player may lead or play a card identical with a card in a declaration on the table, and score the value of that declaration when next he wins a trick. For example, he has a non-trump sequence consisting of ♦ A K Q J 10 on the table; he plays a ♦ Q from his hand and announces 150. If the ♦ Q wins the trick, or the next time the player wins a trick, he may score the 150. It should be noted that this is equivalent to playing the ♦ Q from the table, and then restoring the declaration with the ♦ Q from his hand after next winning a trick.

A marriage may be declared and scored, and on a later turn A-J-10 of the suit may be added and the entire value of the sequence scored; but if the entire sequence is scored first, neither that king nor that queen may thereafter be scored in a marriage.

A card on the table may be used to restore a declaration which has been broken up. For example, a player declares A-K-Q-J-10 and later K-Q of the same suit; upon playing one of the kings, he may score the value of the sequence again, as he is deemed to have played the king from the sequence and then to have restored the sequence with the king from the marriage.

Double bézique declared at one time counts only 500, but single bézique may be declared for 40 and then a second bézique added for an additional 500, provided the first bézique is still on the table. The same principle governs the scoring of triple bézique and quadruple bézique.

The final play. No declaration may be scored after the last two cards of the stock have been drawn. Each player picks up any cards he has on the table, giving him twelve cards in all. The winner of the previous trick leads.

In this final play, the non-leader must follow suit if able, and must win the trick if able, by trumping if necessary.

The winner of the last trick scores 250.

Game. Each deal constitutes a game. The player with the higher total adds 1,000 to his score and his margin of victory is the difference between his score and his opponent's, remainders of less than 100 being disregarded. For example, the winner scores 4,320 and the loser 3,690. The winner receives 4,300 + 1,000 — 3,600, or a net of 1,700.

Rubicon. If the loser has scored less than 3,000, the winner receives all the points scored by both players, plus 1,000 for game, even if the winner's score was also under 3,000. For example, the winner has 2,960 and the loser has 2,930. The winner receives 2,900 + 2,900 + 1,000, a net of 6,800.

Irregularities: *Incorrect deal.* May be rectified by mutual agreement, but either player may demand a new deal. There must be a new deal if either player is dealt too many cards and it is discovered before a card is played.

Incorrect hand. If it is discovered at any time that each player has more than 12 cards, there must be a new deal. If it is discovered, after both players have drawn from the stock, that a player has fewer than 12 cards, play continues and the player with fewer cards than his opponent cannot win the last trick. If one player has too many cards and his opponent the right number, the offender is rubiconed but his score cannot be counted as more than 2,900. If the play is not completed, there is no score for last trick.

Exposed card. Non-dealer may demand a new deal if one of his cards is exposed in dealing. There must be a new deal if a card of the pack is found exposed before a play has been made; if discovered thereafter, the card is shuffled into the stock.

Illegal draw. If a player, in drawing, sees a card he is not entitled to, his opponent at his next draw may look at the two top cards of the stock and select either.

Lead out of turn. Must be withdrawn on demand, but may not be withdrawn without permission.

Odd number of cards in stock. The last card is dead.

Error in declaring. If a player shows and scores for cards which do not in fact constitute the declaration claimed, the score stands unless the opponent demands correction before playing to the next trick.

Error in scoring. May be corrected at any time before the final score for the deal has been agreed.

Revoke. If a player fails to play according to the law after the stock is exhausted, his opponent scores last trick.

Imperfect pack. If discovered before the final score has been agreed, the deal is void; except that if the imperfection consists of a shortage due to cards found on the floor or in the vicinity of the table, the deal stands and such cards are dead.

Looking back at played cards is permitted. Counting the stock to see how many cards remain is permitted.

Variants: The English game of Six-pack Bézique differs in some respects from the American and French forms.

The English count only the combination of ♠ Q and ♦ J as bézique, no matter what suit is trump. As they play, the same suit may become trump in two or more consecutive deals.

The English also count 250 for *carte blanche*. This consists of a hand originally dealt with no picture card in it (that is, consisting wholly of aces, tens, nines, eights and sevens). The holder shows his entire hand and scores the 250. Thereafter, each time he draws a card he may show it, and if it is not a picture card he scores 250 again. In the same turn in which he scores 250 for carte blanche, he may, if he won the trick and has the necessary cards, score 100 for aces, etc. Once he draws a picture card he may no longer score for carte blanche, even if his hand thereafter becomes devoid of picture cards.

Eight-pack Bezique: In some circles, Bézique is played with eight 32-card packs and is supplanting the six-pack game.

The eight-pack game is exactly the same as the six-pack game, described on the preceding pages, except for the increased number of cards and the following differences:

In the deal, each player receives 15 cards.

Single bézique counts 50, double bézique 500, triple bézique 1,500, quadruple bézique 4,500 and quintuple bézique 9,000.

Five trump aces count 2,000, five trump tens 1,800, five trump kings 1,600, five trump queens 1,200 and five trump jacks 800.

The loser is rubiconed if he fails to reach 5,000.

Pointers on Play: If the trump has not been established, and you have a marriage, declare it immediately—

even if you have no other cards of that suit, and have an outside strong suit in which you "may" draw a marriage later.

Lead an ace if you have one (there being no trump, it cannot fail to win). Lead a ten if you lack an ace (your opponent probably will not hold the ace of that suit). Sacrifice even a trump ace if necessary to insure winning the trick. The queen of your marriage gives you at least a start toward a bézique. Delay may permit your opponent to make his own strong suit trumps, and that will often lead to your being rubiconed.

Even toward the late stages, hold on to the queens and jacks which make béziques. There is still time to draw the matching cards and get the high scores.

Be sure to count the trump queens and the bézique jacks carefully. Know when they are all accounted for, so you will not spoil other declaring opportunities to hold on to them.

It is usually worth while to delay declaring four bézique jacks (which count only 40), and even four queens of trumps, which count 600, so as not to let your opponent know that he can no longer draw those cards.

In the play for the last trick, which counts 250 and often determines the winner of the game, length in trumps is important. Therefore, do not waste sevens, eights and nines of trumps to win unimportant tricks in the earlier play. Use cards for trick-winning only when you have a declaration which can no longer be delayed without destroying the prospects of your hand.

Do not hesitate to throw away kings and queens in non-trump suits in order to wait for cards which figure in higher-scoring combinations. Do not hesitate to throw away tens. Do not save cards in the hope of drawing a non-trump sequence at the expense of giving up even a less favorable prospect of completing a higher-scoring declaration.

When only twelve or fourteen cards remain in the stock (six or seven more tricks before the stock is exhausted) stop and figure out what declarations your opponent may be holding. If he may have (or may be likely to get) some important declaration like triple or quadruple bézique, try to prevent his winning a trick — by leading your aces of trumps, if necessary, even though you thereby relinquish your chance at winning the last trick.

KALABRIAS

Why You'll Like It: This is the game of "Klob" that Damon Runyon's tough Broadway characters play, in his celebrated short stories. It's also the same game as Belotte, which is the most popular card game of France. Its principles are strange to American card players, so special care may be required to learn it; but fifty million Frenchmen can't be wrong.

What You Need: The pack of 32 cards, made by discarding all sixes and lower cards from the standard 52-card pack. Also, pencil and paper for scoring.

Let's Play a Game: The pack is shuffled and spread, and you and your opponent each draw a card. Your card is the ♣ 9, his is the ♥ K. Your card being lower, you must deal.

Again you shuffle the pack, let him cut it, and deal two hands of six cards each, three at a time. You turn over the next card of the pack and place it partly underneath the stock when you lay it down. This card proposes the trump suit for the hand.

Your opponent, as non-dealer, bids first. He passes. You look at your hand:

The trump card is the ♥ 8. Your hand is not good enough to warrant your accepting hearts as trumps; your hearts look good, but in this game both ♥ J and ♥ 9 would outrank your ace of hearts if hearts became trumps. But if you pass, he will have a chance to name a different trump suit, at which he will do well, by the looks of your hand. So you say "Schmeiss!" This means "I propose that we abandon this deal, but if you insist, I will become the *maker* with hearts as trumps." By schmeissing you prevent him from naming the trump suit, and stand a chance to avoid having to play a weak hand.

Your opponent says "Yes," acceding to the proposal, so you throw in the cards, your opponent shuffles and deals.

This time you both pass, and once more the cards are gathered and redealt. You deal yourself

KALABRIAS

The turned card is the ♦ A.

Your opponent passes, but you say "I take," meaning that you will insist on playing the hand out with diamonds as trumps. You have become the *maker*.

First you deal out three more cards to each hand, dealing to your opponent first, three at a time as in the original deal. Thus you actually play with a hand of nine cards. After dealing the extra cards, you expose or turn up the bottom card of the stock. This card is no more used in play than the rest of the stock. Its exposure is merely a custom, no doubt based on the theory that non-dealer is likely to glimpse the bottom card, so the dealer is entitled to see it too.

You are now looking at

You have put the ♦ 9 ahead of the ♦ K because it is the second-best trump. The best is the jack of the suit, which you do not hold—and hope he does not!

Although you are the maker, your opponent makes the opening lead, because he is the non-dealer. His card is the ♣ K. Before playing to the lead, you have two things to do.

You announce "Twenty" and show the ♠ 10-9-8. A sequence of three cards in the same suit counts 20; a sequence of four or more counts 50.

In reckoning sequences, the cards rank A (high), K, Q, J, 10, 9, 8, 7. But in trick-taking, the ten ranks just below the ace, and in trumps the jack is moved up to the head of the suit, with the nine next. The jack of trumps, by the way, is called *jasz*, pronounced yahss, and the nine *menel*, pronounced muh-NELL.

If your opponent held a sequence to the ten or higher, he would have announced it before leading, and you could not have counted your spade sequence, for only one player may count for this meld, and the best in the cards wins. But you knew you could show and count your spades because he did not announce any meld before leading.

Having scored your 20, you show your ♦ 7 and exchange it for the turned-up ♦ A. This exchange privilege goes only to the lowest trump, called the *dix* (deece).

Now you are ready to play to the first lead. Having no clubs, you must trump, and you elect to play the ♦ A which you have just obtained. You lead the ♠ Q and he drops the ♠ J. You continue with the ♠ 8, and he wins with the ♠ A. His return of the ♣ 9 forces your ♦ 10, and then he trumps your ♠ 9 with the ♦ Q.

He puts out the ♣ J, and you take with the ♦ 9. You use menel rather than the ♦ K because they are equals (you had the ♦ A-10), but menel counts more in your tricks.

At this juncture you see that if your opponent has the jasz you cannot save your ♠ 10, which is a valuable card. Your only chance is that if he has another trump it is the eight-spot. So you lead your ♦ K and are happy to see him drop the ♦ 8. Then you cash the ♠ 10, on which he drops the ♥ J, and he takes your ♥ Q with the ♥ A.

On running through the cards you have each taken in

KALABRIAS

tricks you find that he has taken 28 points, plus 10 for last trick, a total of 38. (Every ace taken in tricks counts 11; ten, 10; king, 4; queen, 3; jack, 2, except that jasz counts 20 and menel 14.) You have taken 62 points, with a meld of 20, a total of 82. These totals are carried forward on the score sheet. Had you, as maker, failed to score more than he, you would have scored nothing, and he would have scored your count of cards won as well as his own.

Laws of Kalabrias: *Drawing.* Lower card deals. In drawing, the cards rank: A (high), K, Q, J, 10, 9, 8, 7.

Dealing. Dealer must give six cards to each player, three at a time, beginning with his opponent. The next card of the pack must be placed face up on the table. After the trump is decided, dealer must give each hand three more cards, three at a time (or one at a time, if agreed). He must also turn up and set aside the bottom card of the pack.

Bidding. Non-dealer has first turn to bid. He may pass, *take it* (accept the suit of the turned card as trump and thereby become the *maker*), or *schmeiss*. If he passes, dealer has the same three options. The *schmeiss* is a proposal to abandon the deal and have a new deal by the other player. The dealer may agree to or refuse the schmeiss; if he refuses, non-dealer becomes the *maker* with the turned card for trump.

A schmeiss by dealer, following a pass by non-dealer, has the same meaning and effect, and non-dealer may agree or refuse.

If both players pass, non-dealer may again pass, or may schmeiss, or may name any suit as trump except that previously rejected. The schmeiss may be refused by the dealer, in which case the non-dealer must name the trump and become the maker.

If non-dealer passes in the second round, dealer may name the trump suit (other than the rejected suit) or abandon the deal.

Sequence. After the hands are filled to nine cards, but before playing to the first trick, either player holding a *sequence* may score for it. A sequence is three or more cards of adjacent ranks in the same suit, the cards ranking as in drawing for deal. A sequence of three counts 20; of four or more, 50.

If non-dealer holds a sequence, he should indicate the fact by saying "Twenty" or "Fifty" before leading. If dealer has no sequence, or none of equal value, he must say "Good," whereupon non-dealer may score. If dealer has a sequence of greater value, he says "Not good" and scores. If dealer has a sequence of equal value, he must say "How high?" and non-dealer must then name the highest card of his sequence or state that it is in trumps.

A sequence of four or more cards is superior to a sequence of three; between sequences of the same class (50 or 20) the higher in rank is superior; between sequences of the same class and rank, one in trumps is superior to one in a plain suit, and of two in plain suits that held by non-dealer is superior.

Only the player holding the superior sequence may score; if he holds two sequences, he may score both.

All sequences that score must be exposed in full to the opponent. If non-dealer leads without claiming a sequence, before playing to the lead dealer may show and score any sequences he holds.

KALABRIAS

The dix. The player who holds the seven of trumps (called *dix*) may exchange it for the turned card when that suit is accepted by either player for trump. He must make the exchange before he has played to the first trick. Dealer may wait until his opponent has made the opening lead before exchanging.

The play. The opening lead is made by non-dealer, regardless of which player is maker. A lead requires the other hand to follow suit if able, or to trump if void of the suit led. If unable to follow suit or trump, the hand may play any card. A trump lead requires the other hand to play higher if able. A trick is won by the higher trump or by the higher card of the suit led. The winner of a trick leads to the next.

In the play, the cards of the trump suit rank: J (high), 9, A, 10, K, Q, 8, 7. The cards of each plain suit rank: A (high), 10, K, Q, J, 9, 8, 7.

The objects in play are (a) to score for *bella*; (b) to win counting cards in tricks; (c) to win the last trick, which counts 10.

Bella. The combination of the king and queen of trumps counts 20 points for the player to whom it is dealt, regardless of how the cards fall in tricks. It should not be announced in advance of play; when the second of the two cards is played, the owner may announce "Bella" and then score the 20. (It is proper for the maker, if he sees that he will go *bete* even with a score for *bella*, to fail to claim it, and so deprive his opponent of the 20 points.)

Counting cards. The following cards score points for the player who takes them in tricks:

71

In trumps

Jack (*jasz*)	20
Nine (*menel*)	14
Ace	11
Ten	10
King	4
Queen	3

In each plain suit

Ace	11
Ten	10
King	4
Queen	3
Jack	2

Lower cards have no scoring value.

Scoring. After the play, each player adds the points he has scored in the deal by sequence, bella, last trick, and cards won in tricks. If the maker has a higher total than his opponent, each scores what he has made. If the totals are equal, the maker scores nothing, while the opponent scores what he has made. If the opponent has the higher total, he scores the sum of what both players have made.

The first player to reach 500 points wins a game. "Counting out" during play is not allowed. The last deal of a game is played to the finish, and if both reach 500 or more, the higher total wins.

Irregularities. Before bidding, non-dealer may require a new deal if any of his cards or any card left in the stock was exposed in dealing; he may require a new deal or demand correction if either player was dealt the wrong number of cards. When correction is demanded, a hand with too many cards is offered face down to the opponent, who draws out the excess; a short hand is supplied from the top of the stock.

If a hand is discovered to be incorrect after the bidding

has begun, but before it has played to the first trick, it must be corrected as above. If a hand is discovered to be incorrect after it has played to the first trick, the holder is penalized as for a revoke.

A *revoke* is a failure to follow suit when able, or to trump when able, or to play higher when able on a trump lead. If a player revokes and does not correct his error before playing to the next trick, his opponent receives all the points in that deal. The same penalty is applied to a player who is found to have an incorrect number of cards after he has played to the first trick.

Pointers on Play: *When to take.* On the average, a deal contains about 110 points. On the average, the trump maker needs about 60 points to win the deal. To win 60 points with nine cards means, on the average, to win 40 points with six cards. Thus the normal minimum hand for a *take* is one that counts 40 or has strong prospect of winning 40. For example:

With the ♠ Q turned, non-dealer holding this hand should take. The jasz is a sure trick and the two aces are highly probable, making 42.

In valuing a hand to determine whether to take, count the following at full scoring value: jasz, menel, any ace, any sequence, bella. It at once occurs to the astute reader that menel can be caught with the jasz; an ace may be trumped; a sequence may be not good — and so on. The answer is that these catastrophes are extremely rare — much rarer than they have to be to be ignored in hand valuation.

A ten-spot not accompanied by the ace has potential but uncertain value. As a powerful "plus" card, it often swings the scales in favor of any otherwise sub-minimum take. For example:

With the ♠ Q turned, this hand should take.

It is more important to hold jasz or menel than to hold length in the turned trump. The first example shows a take with only one trump, the jasz. It might be added that although 18/32 of the cards are in play on each deal, the jasz is in play well over 18/32 of the time — probably 80% of the time — for the holding of a jack is the strongest single inducement to make that suit trump. Lack of the jasz requires solider values for a take.

Since the average holding in any suit, in the original six cards, is one or two, a length of three cards is a "long suit." This length, plus jasz alone or about 30 points in high cards, justifies a take. For example, look at the two hands at the top of the next page.

Either hand, with ♠ Q turned, should take. There is a clear element of risk, but it is less than lies in letting the opponent name the trump.

A holding of any four or more trumps is a proper take.

It must be recognized that the assignment of 110 points per deal is only an *average* value; in a typical session of Kalabriàs the deals are found to vary from about 75 to 160 points. The bidder is entitled to modify the average bidding requirements in accordance with whether he estimates that the deal will fall well above or well below the average of 110. To take an extreme example:

The trouble with this hand for a take in spades is not so much the absence of a countable 40 points for the maker as the presence of an excessive number of unguarded counting cards, some or all of which must fall in play to the opponent. The deal potentially is "rich," and in any such case the taker should hold an ironclad 40.

Considerable nonsense has been written and talked about the chances of improvement from the draw of three extra cards. Experience as well as abstract probability show the folly of bidding in the hope of catching any specific cards, as an ace to protect a ten—and also the folly of ignoring the fact that *some* strength and counting values are almost sure to be added to a hand. At the very least, the draw should be counted on to supply at least a *guard,* as for a blank ten. And it also considerably decreases the chance that the opponent will hold a void in any plain suit and so be able to trump a plain ace. There is frequently a strong chance that it will create a sequence among "near" cards in the hand, or promote a 20-sequence to a 50. All these possibilities are weighed by the experienced player in judging close takes, and it may be said that, in consequence, his standard minimum for a take is 35 rather than 40.

The schmeiss. It takes but a moment's reflection to see that the non-dealer should never schmeiss in his first turn. If he would prefer another suit as trump, the only way he can get opportunity to name it is to pass. If he is not strong enough to take, he can gain nothing by giving dealer the chance to force him to take, since then the dealer with an ironclad can assure himself of scoring the non-dealer's points as well as his own.

But the schmeiss is a powerful weapon for the dealer. A hand just below the normal minimum for a take calls for a schmeiss. Non-dealer is thereby deprived of the opportunity to name his own trump, and dealer can rest assured that if he is forced to take (by refusal of the schmeiss) the non-dealer probably has as weak a hand in the turned trump as his own. (It is true that non-dealer might try "sand-bagging" by passing a strong hand in the turned trump, waiting for a schmeiss, but on the average the stratagem goes pfut, as dealer passes most of the time.) For example, dealer holds:

With ♠ Q turned, this hand is too weak for a take. Yet it has even less value if any other suit is trump. Dealer should schmeiss.

Similar considerations govern the schmeiss by non-dealer on the second round. For example:

The turned ♠ Q has been rejected. This hand has 34 in sight for a make of hearts, which is sub-par. But non-dealer would rather take a chance on a heart make than hear dealer name clubs or diamonds. He should therefore schmeiss.

The play. The principal question for the maker is whether or when to lead trumps. As a general rule, the jasz should be led at the earliest opportunity, unless it must be retained to protect a tenace. For example, lead the jasz from J-K-8, or J alone, but not from J-A. The object in cashing the high trump is to catch the ace or ten, if possible, and to reduce the adverse trump length available for ruffing your own side cards. But if the second is not a pertinent consideration, it is usually better not to lead trumps, saving them to win the last trick. For example:

Spades are trumps, the ♠ Q being turned. Any side tricks won by this hand go on the first round of the suit. There is no urgency about leading trumps. Lead the ♦ 10 at the first opportunity, make the aces and the ♠ 10 as the occasion arises, save the jasz if possible to make the last trick.

As is shown in this example, a blank ten-spot should be led. It will make in any event only if the opponent does not hold the ace. If he wins, the lead has operated as a safe exit, preserving the side suits in which the hand has a chance to catch something from the opponent.

The best policy for the opponent of the maker is usually to lead his long suit in the hope of forcing the other, sooner or later, to trump. But this policy should be modified if the long suit contains a tenace, as A-K-8, or if the hand is strong enough in trumps to play as though it were the making hand.

KALABRIAS

For both players, the policy indicated when the holdings are broken is to exit by the safest route at each juncture. For example:

Non-dealer has named hearts after his second-round schmeiss was refused. The ♠ Q was rejected on the first round. He should lead the ♠ 9, planning to exit at each turn and make his tens and menel on adverse leads. If the worst happens—dealer leads two more rounds of spades—trump with the ♥ 10, then lead ♣ A and ♣ K. If dealer makes the ♣ 10, at least he has to lead again. Should he have a third club to lead, trump with menel and lead ♥ 8.

CASINO

Why You'll Like It: So simple that it is the first card game taught to most children . . . so rich in opportunity for skilful play that hardened professional gamblers compete in Casino games for the highest stakes—here is a game that is favored by all ages and groups. For children it is admirable training in arithmetic and analytical thinking. Grown-ups can, if they will, carry the process of analysis much farther.

What You Need: A standard 52-card pack, with pencil and paper for keeping score.

Let's Play a Game: You and your opponent each draw a card from the pack. Your card is the ♣ 5; his is the ♥ J. As your card is lower, you deal first.

You shuffle the pack and let your opponent cut it. Then you deal him two cards at once. The next two cards you turn face up on the table. Then you deal yourself two cards at once. You repeat this round of the deal, so that each of you has four cards and there are four face up on the table.

CASINO

Suppose that the cards in sight to you are

On the table:

In your hand:

Your opponent plays first, since you dealt. He lays the ♥ 7 from his hand on the ♠ 7 and *takes them in* — puts them face down near himself.

Now you could take in the ♦ 3 with your ♥ 3, but instead you take in the ♦ 3 and ♥ 6 with your ♣ 9, as you may do because they add to nine. You preferred this play because it gave you three cards instead of two, and you want to try to win the majority of the cards.

Your opponent then *trails* with the ♦ K—lays it face up on the table without taking anything in. As you cannot take in anything either, you trail with the ♥ 5. Your opponent takes in the ♦ K with the ♠ K. You then lay the ♥ 3 on the ♥ 5, saying "Eight." You may make this *build* because you have in your hand an eight with which you can take in the 5-3 at your next turn. But unfortunately your opponent's last card is the ♣ 8, so he takes your build, and you have to lay down your ♦ 8 without getting anything for it.

The cards being gone from your hands, two new hands are dealt. You give four cards to your opponent and four to yourself, two at a time, but now you do not give any cards to the table. Each time the hands are played out, you will deal eight more cards in the same way. When you come to the last eight cards of the pack, be sure to announce "Last deal."

After the second deal the cards you see are

On the table:

In your hand:

Your opponent puts the ♣ A from his hand on the ♦ 8, saying "Nine," for an ace is 1 in building. Now, you might take in the ♠ Q, but you would rather get the ace if you can, for aces are valuable. Also, if possible you want to save your own ace and also your ♦ 10, which is *Big Casino*, the most valuable of all cards. So you put the ♥ A on his build and say "Ten." You may *increase a build* with a card from your hand—whether it is your opponent's build or your own.

CASINO

Only your ♦ 10 (or another ten) will take this build. Face cards do not have any numerical value. A face card may be used only to take in a like face card—and only one at a time. If there is a queen on the table and you have two queens in your hand, you may not "build queens."

Happily your opponent does not have a ten, so he trails with the ♠ 9. You take in the build with the ♦ 10. He trails with the ♦ J, and you take in the ♠ Q with your ♥ Q. He trails the ♠ 4, which you take in with the ♣ 4.

Play continues in the same way, with hands of four cards dealt until the pack is run through.

After the hands are played out in the last deal, any cards remaining on the table belong to the player who was last to take in any cards. Now let's see what we are trying to win during the play.

The Points: After the play, you compare the packet of cards you have won with your opponent's packet. If necessary, one of you counts his packet to see who has most cards. Then one of you counts the spades he has taken in. You both note how many aces you have, and who captured the ♦ 10 and the ♠ 2. Finally, you note the sweeps, if any. The points that count are as follows:

Cards, for taking 27 or more cards	3
Spades, for taking 7 or more spades	1
Big Casino, the ♦ 10	2
Little Casino, the ♠ 2	1
Aces, 1 for each ace taken in	4
Sweeps, 1 for each	

A *sweep* is scored whenever a player clears the table of all remaining cards. It is marked by turning a card face up in the pile of cards taken in.

Exclusive of sweeps there are 11 points to be won. Actually, it is only necessary for one of you to count his points. The other need only count his sweeps.

If you wish, you may treat each deal as a separate game, won by the player who makes the higher number of points. But the usual practice is to play for 21 points. If both of you reach 21 in the same deal, the points are counted in the order given above, and the first then to make 21 wins. In some circles *counting out* is permitted. If a player during the play takes in enough points to reach 21 and announces the fact, he wins at once and the deal is not played out.

Laws of Casino: *Dealing.* The player who draws the lower card deals first. Thereafter the deal alternates. A turn to deal consists in giving out the cards until all 52 cards of the pack have been won in play. At the beginning of a turn, each player receives four cards and the table four, dealt two at a time. Thereafter, each player receives four cards, two at a time, but no additional cards are dealt to the table. The dealer must announce "Last" in giving out the last eight cards of the pack.

The Play. Non-dealer always plays first, and thereafter each plays alternately until the hands are exhausted. At each turn, a player must *trail,* or *take in,* or *build,* or *increase a build.*

Face cards may be taken in only by *pairing.* Other cards may be taken in by pairing or *building.* Both pairs and builds may be *duplicated.* For example, a player may place ♥ 7 on the ♣ 7 on the table, announcing "Sevens," and later take in the build with the ♠ 7 or ♦ 7. All three cards of a rank may be taken by the fourth card.

Face cards may not be duplicated in pairing.

CASINO

An example of duplicating a build:

Dealer holds:

On the table:

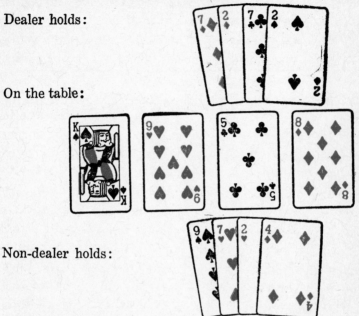

Non-dealer holds:

Non-dealer puts the ♦ 4 on ♣ 5 and covers with ♥ 9, announcing "Nines." Dealer trails with the ♦ 7. Non-dealer adds it to his build with the ♥ 2 from his hand. Dealer trails with ♠ 2. Non-dealer adds it to the build with the ♥ 7 from his hand. Dealer trails with ♠ 2. Non-dealer finally takes his quadrupled build with the ♠ 9.

A player may make a build only if he holds in his hand a card able to take it in. The announcement made by the builder governs what card can take it; for example, if a player puts a five on a five and says "Ten," his opponent may not take it with a five.

A build may be duplicated (any number of times) by cards from the table, but may be *increased* only by a card from the hand. Even when a card is added from the hand on a build, no card from the table may be added as well to make the new total, but a card from the table may be added if it duplicates the increased build. For example, a player may place an ace on a build of six to make seven, but he could not also add a two from the table to make nine. But he could add a seven already on the table, to duplicate the increased build.

A build duplicated in any way may not be increased.

A player may increase his own build, as well as an adverse build.

Having a build on the table (or having been last to increase a build) a player at his next turn may not *trail*. He must play upon his build, or take it in, or take in other cards.

Scoring. Points to be scored are as follows:

Cards, for taking 27 or more cards	3
Spades, for taking 7 or more spades	1
Big Casino, the ♦ 10	2
Little Casino, the ♠ 2	1
Aces, 1 for each ace taken in	4
Sweeps, 1 for each	
	—
	11

The first to reach a total of 21 points wins a game. Points are counted in the order given by the table, to determine the winner if both can reach 21 in the same deal. If the aces decide, they are counted, in order, spades, clubs, hearts, diamonds. If counting out is allowed by agreement, the first to make a correct claim that he has reached 21 wins the game.

Casino

Irregularities: A card played out of turn must remain on the table, and the player misses his next turn. This applies also to an illegal trail when a player has a build on the table; on demand, he must take his build, but the card illegally trailed remains.

If a player attempts to take in cards to which he is not entitled, he must retract his play on demand, but if his opponent plays before drawing attention to the error, the incorrect play stands without penalty.

If a player makes a build and is then found to lack any card that can take it in, his opponent may add one point to his own score or deduct one point from the offender's score, and the cards of the false build are spread and all become available.

Pointers on Play: It is very easy to *play at* Casino. If you want to be an expert, you must above all else *train your memory*. In the last deal, you should know the rank of every card held by your oponent. At every stage before that, you should know how many cards of each rank are still to come. This is not so difficult as it sounds, because happily you do not have to bother about the suits.

In the early play, do not avoid building with aces and Little Casino for fear that your opponent will take the build. Your chances of saving these low cards are better by building than by trailing. At a late stage of play, your knowledge of what cards are left may occasionally show you that trailing is safer. If you are non-dealer, and no better course offers, save a *cash point* card (ace or Little Casino) for your last trail, as you may be able to take it in your first play of the next deal.

Beware of building a pair, when you have a third of the same rank, if there are some middling or low cards on the table, and especially if you have another eight, nine or ten. To get one extra card, you have committed yourself to the build. At your next turn you may wish you were free to make another build.

Take low cards in preference to high cards from the table, in order to minimize the building opportunities for your opponent. When feasible, avoid trailing with a card that allows ten to be built from the table, so long as Big Casino has not appeared.

Taking in a face card is usually a safe, non-committal play, but not if it leaves the possibility of a sweep open to your opponent. And in the last deal, save a face card that pairs with one on the table, to the last, so as to try for the table cards if you need them to score for majority.

When dealt a pair of aces, or a pair of deuces including Little Casino, and your other cards give little hope of using them in a high build, your best chance is to let your opponent deplete the table. Trail with your lowest remaining card, and hold back until he has made a build or taken some of the cards from the table. Then trail a card of your pair. By that time there may be nothing left with which he can build it.

Keep track of cards and spades. In the early play, naturally take a spade in preference to another card, if other considerations do not supervene. But you don't want to strain for cards or spades after you have won a majority.

RUSSIAN BANK

Why You'll Like It: This is perhaps the most popular two-hand game played in the United States, and for a good reason: Interest in every game continues to the very end. It is almost impossible for one player to be so far behind that he must abandon hope of winning. The opponent may be down practically to his last card, while you have scarcely started, and you can still run out the game on him.

In mechanics, Russian Bank is very similar to the principal solitaire games and is quickly learned by anyone who plays solitaire.

What You Need: Two standard 52-card packs, with different backs.

Let's Play a Game: You start by spreading one pack face down and each drawing a card. You draw the ♥ 7, and he the ♣ 10. As your card is lower, you will have first turn.

You each shuffle one pack—the pack to be used by the other fellow. Then, having swapped packs, you each deal your part of the *layout*.

First count off twelve cards face down from the top of your pack, and put them on the table at your right. This is your *stock*. Next deal four cards face up in a column above your stock, extending toward your opponent. This column, together with the similar column dealt by your opponent, forms the *tableau*. The space between the two columns is the *center*, where you will later place all eight aces in two columns. Finally, leave the balance of your pack on the table at your left, forming your *hand*.

Meanwhile your opponent has dealt his pack in the same manner. The complete layout is depicted on the opposite page. The cards whose faces are shown are the *tableau*. Aligned with the columns of the tableau, face down, are the *stocks* and *hands*. The broken lines show the *center* piles and the *talons*, which are yet to be started.

You start the play by moving the ♦ A from the tableau to the center. The aces are the *foundations*, which are to be built up in suit and sequence to the king. Next you put the ♦ 2 on the ♦ A—any play to the foundations must be made first.

The center being "satisfied," you turn to building in the tableau. You put the ♠ J on the ♥ Q—bulding down and in alternating colors. Then the ♦ 10 will go on the ♠ J. Altogether you now have four *spaces* in the tableau, which must be restored to eight piles sooner or later.

As you must fill these spaces from your stock (so long as it lasts), you commence turning up cards from the top of your stock one by one. They come up in this order:

RUSSIAN BANK

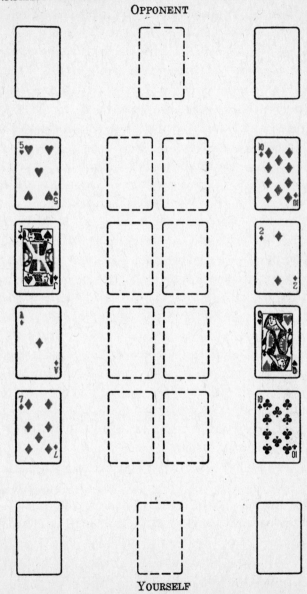

♠ 6 (build it on the ♦ 7, then put the ♥ 5 on it, making a fifth space) ; ♣ A (place in the center) ; ♥ K (goes in a space) ; ♠ 8 (goes in a space; unmake the pile you have just built on the ♦ 7 by putting the ♥ 5 and ♠ 6 in spaces, then rebuild the whole from ♦ 7 down on the ♠ 8, leaving four spaces) ; ♣ 7 (goes in a space) ; ♥ 10 (goes in a space) ; ♦ 3 (build in the center on ♦ 2) ; ♠ 2 (goes in a space) ; ♠ 3 (goes in a space) ; ♥ 4.

As the tableau spaces are all filled, and there is no place to build the ♥ 4, you leave it on top of your stock and turn up the top card of your *hand*. It is the ♣ 2; put it on the ♣ A. The next card from your hand is the ♣ J. As there is no place for it in the layout, place it face up between your hand and stock, commencing your *talon* or *waste pile*. Putting the card on the talon ends your turn. The appearance of the layout now is shown on the opposite page.

As no play to the center is possible, your opponent turns up the top card of his stock before deciding what to do. It proves to be the ♣ J. He puts the ♣ 10 from the tableau on your talon card, which is the other ♣ J, then puts his ♣ J on it— the dog! You want to get rid of as many cards as you can, and here he has *loaded* you with some additional cards. Loading goes by suit and sequence, but the sequences can go up or down—or both ways!

He could similarly load the ♥ 5 from the tableau on the ♥ 4 on your stock, but he does not do so—yet. One reason for deferring this possible play is that, if the ♠ 6 is still clear when it comes your turn, you can simply put the ♥ 5 back on it.

RUSSIAN BANK

The next card he turns from his stock is the ♠ 4, and he put it in the space. Then he turns the ♥ 10, which is unplayable. From his hand comes the ♣ Q, which he adds to your talon. The next is the ♠ A, which goes in the center, and he hastens to build the ♠ 2 and ♠ 3 upon it. When he turns up the ♥ A from his hand, you triumphantly call "Stop!" He has made an error in procedure and so loses his turn. He should have played the ♠ 4 from the tableau to the center before returning to his hand. His turn ends, and you take over.

You make the play of the ♠ 4, then put the ♥ 4 from your stock into the space. You now have a good head start on him. What you are trying to do is to get rid of all the cards from your stock, hand and talon upon the tableau and center piles. The first to get rid of his cards wins.

Laws of Russian Bank: Procedure of dealing and play was set forth in the illustrative game preceding this section.

Stops. A player may be stopped, and he loses his turn, if he violates any of the following rules as to the order of play:

1. A play to the center must be made before any other, except that after his first turn a player is entitled to see the top card of his stock before making any play at all. If the uppermost card of a tableau pile can be played to the center, it must be so played. But it is not compulsory to uncover lower cards by manipulations of the tableau, in order to play to the center.

2. If the stock card can be played to the center, it must be so played before a play from tableau to center. If several

tableau cards can be moved to the center, the player may move them in any order he pleases.

3. Spaces in the tableau may be used for manipulating. The uppermost card of any tableau pile may be moved into a space. But all spaces in the tableau must be filled before a card is turned from the hand. They must be filled from the stock until that is exhausted, after which they may be filled from the hand.

4. Loading the adverse stock or hand may be executed at any time, so long as no play to the center is possible.

5. Having turned a card from his hand, the player may place it on his hand pile momentarily in order to make some manipulation that will make this card playable (as, loading the adverse stock). But if the card from the hand is laid on the talon, the player's turn ends.

Playable cards. The uppermost card of a tableau pile, the top card of the stock, and the card turned from the hand, are always available to be moved elsewhere. The top card of the talon is never so available.

An available card may be placed on a center pile if it matches in suit and ascending sequence; on a tableau pile if it is of opposite color and descending sequence; on the adverse stock or talon, if it matches in suit and sequence in either direction; or in any space of the tableau.

The talon. A player may spread his own talon to examine the cards; if he does so, his opponent also is entitled to see the cards. But a player may not spread his opponent's talon without permission.

When the hand is exhausted, the talon is turned over and becomes a new hand.

Scoring. The player who first gets rid of all cards from

his stock, hand and talon wins, and scores 30 points for winning the game, plus 2 points for each card left in the adverse stock, plus 1 point for each card left in the adverse hand and talon. (Some do not give a bonus for winning; others make the bonus more or less than 30.)

Irregularities: If a player touches a card except for the stated purpose of arranging, such act is construed as an intention to turn or move that card, and if the play is out of order, he may be stopped therefor.

When a stop is called, the out-of-order play attempted must be retracted, but if the error was in turning a card from stock or hand, the opponent may direct whether such card shall be left face up or turned down.

If a player makes an incorrect build, as ♠ 7 on ♣ 8, the move must be retracted on demand, but the player may not be stopped therefor. If another move is permitted before correction is demanded, the incorrect pile remains unchanged, but the error may not be repeated. If the incorrect pile is broken up, it may not be restored.

A stop may not be called for an erroneous play if the offender has completed another play thereafter before attention is drawn to the error.

If a player exposes or sees the face of a card in his stock or hand, other than one regularly turned, he may complete his current play but then his turn ends.

Etiquette. It is essential that the player turn each card from his stock or hand by lifting it from the end nearer his opponent, so that his opponent may see its face as he turns it. A player should not, in the effort to avoid errors of procedure, play so slowly that the game becomes boresome for his opponent.

RUSSIAN BANK

Pointers on Play: Russian Bank requires constant attention to the cards. You can lessen the nervous strain by adopting a systematic procedure and making it habitual. First of all, learn to examine the cards in order: center, stock, talon. Whenever a new card becomes available, look at the center to see if it can be played there. Whenever a card is played on a center pile, look for the next card in ascending sequence, on the stock, hand and tableau, to see if it is available or can be released. Whenever the card turned from the hand is played, look not only to the center but also to the stock to see if the stock card has become playable.

The prime objective in early play is to get cards off your stock as quickly as possible. Pay special attention to manipulating the tableau so as to make spaces. Some players adopt the rule that a player can be stopped for failing to make a space when he could, but the injury he does himself seems to be sufficient punishment.

Don't be hasty in loading your opponent. You may regret putting a card out of play that could have been used to prolong your turn. Load when you can thereby make a space or uncover a helpful card. Before ending your turn, look to see if you can load the opponent's talon to advantage. There is no use in loading his stock at this time, since he can immediately unload it.

CRIBBAGE

Why You'll Like It: Cribbage is the most English of all games. It originated in England (Sir John Suckling, the Cavalier poet of the 17th century, is said to have been its inventor) and is played in all English-speaking countries. Its theme is not borrowed from French, Italian and Spanish games, as are those of other games we play. Cribbage is a member of no "family" of games. There is no other game like it.

What You Need: A standard 52-card pack, and a cribbage board. This board is useful in scoring many games, and almost indispensable for Cribbage. The illustration shows what it looks like. There are 30 holes in each long row. You score by use of two pegs, advancing one hole for each point you win. You start at the end of the board containing the extra holes, called *game holes*, count away from it on the outside row of 30, then back on the inside row, ending at the game hole. Thus it takes 61 points to go *once around*, and 121 to go *twice around*.

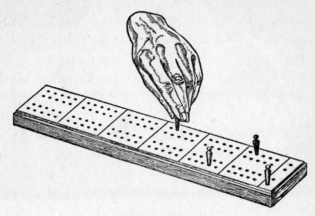

CRIBBAGE BOARD

Let's Play a Game: Let us draw cards to see who deals first. We can follow the Bridge style of spreading the pack in a fan, then drawing cards. But the traditional way of drawing in Cribbage is to lift a packet off the top of the pack and show the bottom card of the packet.

Your card is the ♥ Q, while your opponent shows the ♠ 6. As his card is lower, he deals first.

He shuffles the cards and you cut them. Then he deals two hands of six cards each, one at a time.

Your hand proves to be

Here the cards are arranged by suits, but a better arrangement is by rank. The suits are ignored, except in the one case of a *flush* (explained later).

You each now have to discard two cards, which will go to the *crib*. The crib is in effect an extra hand formed by the four discards, and it counts for the dealer. Since the crib this time will go to your opponent, you want to try to give him *balking cards* while saving the best for yourself. Your hand offers no problem, because it holds one of the best balking combinations, together with a fine scoring combination. So you *lay away* to the crib the ♠ K and ♦ 4, keeping 8-7-7-6.

Your opponent likewise having laid away to the crib, you now cut the pack by lifting a packet off the top. He draws off the top card of the lower packet, you replace the top packet, and he turns the card face up on it. This turned card is the *starter*. It proves to be the ♣ J. Your opponent announces "Two for his heels" and *pegs* two. That is, on his side of the cribbage board he advances a peg two holes away from the *game end*. The bonus of *two for his heels* goes to the dealer when the starter is a jack.

As you are non-dealer, you must play first. You place the ♦ 7 face up on the table, saying "Seven." He lays down the ♦ Q, saying "Seventeen"—the total of the two cards played. All face cards count ten, aces one, other cards their pip value. Each of you keeps possession of his own cards, by playing them in a pile near you.

You play the ♥ 6, calling "Twenty-three." He adds the ♠ 3, calling "Twenty-six." You now have to say "Go," which means that you cannot play another card without carrying the total beyond 31. He then lays down the ♦ 2 and ♣ A, counting to twenty-nine, announces "Go and a run" and pegs 4 points. The *go* counts 1, and the sequence, or *run* of three cards, 3-2-A, played in succession count 3 —one for each card.

As his cards are all gone, you play your last two cards, counting "Eight; fifteen; two and one for go" and peg 3 points. The go for playing the last card counts 1, and the reaching of total *fifteen* scores 2.

In the play of the cards, you have pegged 3 and your opponent 4. Now comes the *showing*—the counting of scores in the hands and crib. As non-dealer, you show first. You spread your hand and count thus: "Fifteen-two; fifteen-four; and double run makes 12." You move your rearmost peg 12 points beyond the peg with which you earlier scored 3. That brings your total score to 15.

What you meant by this rigmarole is: The combination of the ♣ 8 and ♦ 7 adds to fifteen; so does the combination of the ♣ 8 with the ♠ 7; each such group that totals fifteen scores 2 points. You have a run in the ♣ 8 - ♦ 7 - ♥ 6, worth 3 points, and another run by substituting the ♠ 7 for the ♦ 7. Finally, the pair of sevens counts 2 points. A *double run* such as you hold always counts 8—3 points each for two runs and 2 points for the pair.

You were entitled to include the starter, the ♣ J, in counting your hand, as though you held all five cards. But unfortunately the starter added nothing to the count in your hand.

Your opponent now counts his hand, which is Q-3-2-A. He says "Fifteen-two; fifteen-four; and a run is seven." The 3-2 with the queen make one fifteen, and make the other with the starter, the ♣ J. His total score is now 11.

Finally, he turns up his crib, which has hitherto been face down and has not been used in play. The cards are K-9-6-4. He counts "Fifteen—and I give them to myself." He was unlucky to get no additional score out of the two cards you gave him and the starter. His total score is now 13.

Now it is your turn to deal and have the advantage of the crib. The game proceeds by alternate deals, until one of you reaches 61 or 121 points, according as you have agreed to play *once around* or *twice around*.

Laws of Cribbage: *The Deal.* Cards are drawn to determine first deal. The lower card deals first. If cards of equal rank are drawn, both must draw again. Dealer shuffles last. The cut must leave at least four cards in each packet. The deal alternates.

Cards must be dealt one at a time, each player receiving six. Two cards must then be discarded from each hand, face down, to the crib, which belongs to the dealer.

The Play. Non-dealer cuts the pack and dealer turns up the top card of the lower portion as the *starter*, which is placed on top of the pack. If it is a jack, dealer pegs 2 for *his heels*.

Non-dealer leads first by placing a card face up on the table in front of him. Play proceeds, one card at a time, alternately. With each card, its player announces the count of pips reached in that series of plays, aces counting 1 each, face-cards 10 each, other cards their pip value. Any card in the hand may be played at any time, except that the total of cards played in a series may not be carried beyond 31. If unable to play without going over 31, a player must say

CRIBBAGE

go, and the opponent pegs 1 for the go, but must first play additional cards if he can and stay under 32. A go scored by making exactly 31 counts 2.

The opponent of the player who scores for go must make the next lead, unless he has no more cards.

During the play a player who completes any of the following combinations among cards played *consecutively* scores as indicated:

Fifteen. For reaching a total of fifteen, peg 2.

Pairs. For making a pair, peg 2. For making three of a kind, peg 6. For making four of a kind, peg 12. (*Tenth cards*—face cards and tens—pair strictly by rank, e. g. two jacks or two queens, but not a jack and a queen.)

Run. For making a run of three or more cards, peg 1 for each card. (A run counts even if the cards are not played in sequential order, as 5-4-3, so long as no foreign card intervenes, e. g., 6-8-5-4 is not a run because the 8 is foreign, but the play of a 7 would then make a run of five.)

Showing. After the play, the hands are *shown* or counted in order: non-dealer, dealer's hand, crib. The first player to reach 61 or 121 (as agreed) wins the game. If *lurch* is played by agreement, a player is lurched if he has less than 31 or 61 respectively when his opponent wins, and he loses a double game.

In showing, the starter is deemed to be a part of each hand and the crib. Combinations that count are as follows:

Fifteen. Each different combination of two or more cards that totals 15 scores 2.

Pair. Each different combination of two cards of the same rank scores 2.

Run. Each different combination of three or more cards

in sequence scores 1 for each card in the sequence.

Flush. Four cards of the same suit in the hand score 4. Four cards of the same suit in hand or crib of same suit as the starter score 5. (No score for four-flush in the crib.)

His nobs. A jack of the same suit as the starter, in hand or crib, scores 1.

The total count claimed for a hand or crib must be announced, for the opponent's verification. If *muggins* is played by agreement, any score in play or showing overlooked by the one who earns it may be claimed by his opponent.

Irregularities: A player who fails to play when able may not correct his error after the next card is played. The card or cards he erroneously withheld are dead as soon as the error is discovered; the offender may not play them nor peg with them, and his opponent pegs 2 for the error.

There is no penalty for announcing a wrong total of cards, or making a wrong claim of score, but the error must be corrected on demand. But any such error stands as announced if correction is not demanded before the next card is played.

If a player places a peg short of the amount to which he is entitled, he may not correct his error after he has played his next card. If he pegs more than his announced score, the error if proved must be corrected on demand at any time before the cut for the next deal, and his opponent pegs 2 for the error.

Pointers on Play: On picking up your hand, count what you could score with all six cards. Many times this will show what to discard, because there will be only one way to preserve the count in four cards. For example: 10-7-6-6-4-2. There are two fifteens and a pair, in the 7-6-6-2. The 10-4 add nothing to the count, so should be laid away either to your own or opponent's crib.

If you have to break up some scoring combination to discard, two factors have to be considered: (a) whose is the crib; (b) what prospects of improvement by the starter remain after alternative discards. For example: Q-J-9-8-7-5. The hand has three fifteens and a run, but something will have to go. If you are dealer, the right discard is the Q-5. This way you lose only one fifteen (J-5), and keep the run intact. Generally speaking, runs should be saved rather than fifteens, because they offer the best prospect of improvement. Of course the jack is kept with the run, rather than the queen, in case the starter is a ten. If your opponent has the crib, this hand is a headache. To give a five to his crib is dangerous, because there are 16 *tenth* cards in the pack. Best is to keep Q-J-5 for a count of 4, with fair prospect of improvement; for the fourth card keep the 8 in order to *balk* as much as possible. *Near* cards such as 9-7 are dangerous to give to the adverse crib—but you can't do everything!

Middle cards—ranks 5 to 9—are more likely to be saved by both players than high or low cards. Therefore the opening lead of a middle card is dangerous unless the hand is prepared to counter with a score if the opponent makes a pair or fifteen. For example: Q-7-7-5. To lead a seven risks letting the opponent make fifteen—he is likely to have saved an eight if he was dealt one. A better lead is the queen. Although the lead of a tenth card is considered dubious, it is not bad when the leader holds a five. If the opponent makes fifteen, this hand can retort with a pair. If the opponent makes a pair of queens, this hand has a good chance for a go by playing a seven.

With a good hand of middle cards, however, the rule is to *play on*, that is, offer the opponent opportunity to peg so as to retort with an equal or greater score. For example: 8-7-7-4. Here the lead of a seven is good. The hand will peg if opponent makes a fifteen or a pair.

After an adverse lead, it is usually best to make a score if able, even at the risk that the opponent will also score. When unable to score, you may have the question of whether to *play on* or *play off*. The question is decided in the same way as the choice of lead. For example: J-8-8-4. If your opponent leads a 6, don't play an 8, for if he plays a 7 to make a run you cannot counter. Play the jack.

If you and your opponent are both close to game, say 7 points away, play to the score. If it is your deal, save the best possible hand for pegging—let the hand count go. Your opponent shows first, and the average value of a hand is about 7 points. Your hope is to peg out—and as dealer you are bound to peg at least one. But if it is your opponent's deal, save cards that will surely count 7 points or have the best chance of improvement to that total, and play off as far as possible.

EIGHTS

Why You'll Like It: A child can learn this game in
less than a minute . . . it can be played seriously or idly,
and enjoyed either way . . . yet it offers so much scope for
skill that it is a favorite game of champion Contract Bridge
players. Some call the game "Crazy Eights." Others, for no
understandable reason, call it "Swedish Rummy."

What You Need: A standard 52-card pack, and pencil
and paper for scoring.

Let's Play a Game: You spread the pack and you and
your opponent each draw a card. Your card is the ♦ 9,
his the ♠ A. As his is lower, he deals first. After he shuffles
the pack and you cut, he deals two hands of seven cards
each, one at a time. The rest of the pack or *stock* is placed
between you on the table, face down. He turns up the top
card, which proves to be the ♣ 8. Because an eight-spot
is banned as the *starter* he buries it in the middle of the
stock, and turns the next card. This is the ♠ 6. He places
it face up beside the stock.

You look at your hand:

All eight-spots are *wild,* so you had better tuck that ♥ 8 on the other side of the ♠ J, to remind you not to play it as an ordinary heart.

You want to get rid of all your cards, by playing them on the starter. You have to play a card that matches the starter, either in suit or rank. On the ♠ 6 you can play either the ♠ J or the ♦ 6 (it being your first turn to play, as non-dealer). As you have more diamonds than spades, you choose the ♦ 6. He then plays the ♦ 10, you the ♦ 7, he the ♣ 7, and you the ♣ 5.

At this point he evidently has no more clubs and no five-spots, for he draws the top card of the stock. Evidently this is not playable either, for he draws two more before he plays the ♣ 9.

Now you are stuck, having no clubs and no nines. You could play the ♥ 8, for eight-spots are playable at any time, but you decide to save this valuable card for the moment and take your chances on drawing. You get the ♥ K, ♠ 2 and ♠ 9, the last of which is playable. He adds the ♠ Q, you the ♠ J, he the ♥ J, you the ♥ K, he the ♥ 10, you the ♥ A, he the ♠ A, and you the ♠ 2.

EIGHTS

Now he draws again from the stock, and is lucky in getting the ♠ 5 on the first draw. You have only two cards left, the ♥ 8 and ♦ 2. Instead of drawing for a spade or a five, you play the ♥ 8 and say "Diamonds." Whenever an eight-spot is played, the owner can make it call for any suit he pleases (not a rank). The other must then positively play a card of that suit, or else another eight.

Your opponent, with only two cards left, obediently plays the ♦ 4, and then you *go out* by playing the ♦ 2. As you got rid of your cards first, you score all the points remaining in his hand. You didn't get much on this deal—only 3 points for the ♥ 3 he has left (see the rules of *Scoring*). These points are credited to you on the score sheet.

Now it's your turn to deal the next hand. In this manner you will continue until one of you wins the game by amassing a total of 100 points.

Laws of Eights: *The draw.* Low card deals first. Ace ranks at all times below the deuce.

The deal. Each hand receives seven cards, dealt one at a time, beginning with non-dealer. The turn to deal alternates.

The starter. The top card of the stock is turned for the starter. If it is an eight-spot, it must be buried, and a new card turned.

The play. Each player in turn, commencing with non-dealer, must play one card upon the starter pile. The card played must match the top of the pile in either suit or rank, or be an eight-spot. If unable to play at all in turn, a player must draw cards from the top of the stock until able. It is permissible to draw from the stock even though able to play at once. After the stock is exhausted, each player must play whenever able; if one is unable to play, the other plays two or more times in succession until the first can play.

An eight-spot may be played at any time, regardless of whether the hand could play another card. In playing an eight, the owner must announce a suit, and his opponent must then play either a card of that suit or another eight.

Scoring. The first to get rid of all his cards wins the hand, and scores for cards still held by his opponent: 10 for each face card or ten-spot, 1 for each ace, 50 for each eight-spot, the pip value of each other card. The first to reach a total of 100 points wins a game, for which he scores 100 points plus the difference of the two totals.

If the play of a deal ends in a block, neither player being able to play, the hand with the lower total of points wins the difference of the totals.

Irregularities: There must be a new deal by the same dealer if a card is exposed in dealing, or if the wrong number of cards is dealt to either hand.

There is no penalty for passing when able to play, if play continues, but if a player passes and thereby induces his opponent to expose his hand in belief that the game is blocked, the offender may not score in that deal. Play continues, without rectification of the error, and any points finally left in the hand of the offender go to his opponent.

Pointers on Play: As was illustrated in the example game, in the beginning it is advisable to keep as many suits in the hand as possible, and therefore to play from a long suit when able. But circumstances change quickly if there is any drawing. If your opponent has had to draw to get, e.g., a spade, you may well play your last spade in the hope of forcing him to draw again, rather than switch suits.

One eight in the hand should as a rule be saved until the hand is down to two or three cards, even at the cost of drawing. How far to dig depends of course on how many cards the opponent has in his hand. If he has only two or three, be wary of digging too deep, and be quick to unload your eight before you get stuck with it.

Keep track of the number of cards of each suit played. If you cannot keep the exact figures in mind, at least note which suits are nearest to exhaustion. It is by no means a disadvantage to have to draw ten or twenty cards, for you may thereby get a "corner" on the remaining cards of a suit and thus force your opponent to dig several times later. In fact, experienced players often dig deep for eights or "case cards" even when they can play without digging. Of course, such policy depends on keeping track of the cards accurately, so as to be able to unload cards later while keeping the opponent blocked.

Watch especially for the chance to force a block through exhaustion of a suit and also eights. If you have the last eight, and can count thirteen cards of any suit in the starter pile and your hand together, you know you can force your opponent to take the rest of the stock by playing your eight and calling for the exhausted suit. Whether to do so depends on whether the game will end then and there, and whether, if you will still be able to play, you will have let your opponent unload too much.

MILL

Why You'll Like It: Here is Europe's most popular board game. Every schoolboy knows it over there, just as American schoolboys know Checkers. It's simple, too; you'll learn it in a minute. The Mill is an ancient game, known under many other names (Nine Men's Morris, Morelles, and others) and its history is an ancient one—Shakespeare knew it, and the Vikings of Lief Ericsson's time, and the ancient Greeks; the Mill board is cut into a step on the Acropolis at Athens.

What You Need: A board, as shown in the illustration, and nine counters for each player.

The board can be drawn on a large sheet of paper. The numbers are not necessary for play, being added here merely for reference. For pieces, a checker set may be used.

Let's Play a Game: By the flip of a coin it is decided that you will play first. You take the nine "white" pieces and your oponent the nine "black." (In most checker sets the pieces are actually red and black, as in the illustrations

MILL

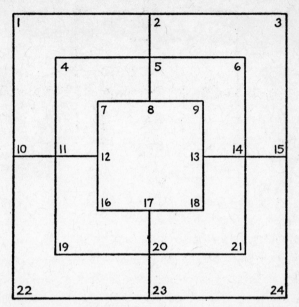

here.) The first phase of the game will be to lay your pieces down on the intersections of the board, one at a time alternately. The object is to get three in a row on a line. Making one *mill*, as it is called, does not win the game at once, but is a start toward victory.

You play your first piece on square 5. Common sense says, seize first the points from which the most lines branch. Your opponent puts his first piece on square 14. Then you take 20 and he takes 11. All very orthodox.

Next you play on 2, threatening to make a mill by taking 8, so he at once plays there to block you. Your next play is on 17, and again he blocks at 23. The position at this juncture is shown in the first diagram on the next page.

Instead of forcing further, you decide to take 12. He sees a chance to force a mill by a *fork* and proceeds to do it. He

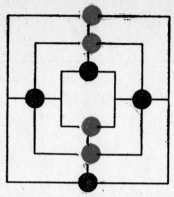

takes 13 and you block at 15. By playing 9 he makes the fork, since you cannot block at 7 and 18 simultaneously. You block at 7, and he makes his mill at 18.

Each time you make a mill, you are entitled to remove one adverse piece from the board, provided that it is not part of a mill. Pieces so removed are out of play forever, and the winner of a game is the one who first reduces the other to only two men.

He removes your man at 7 and you have to play back on the same square to prevent his making a second mill. Then he blocks at 16. You put your last man on 1, and he blocks at 3.

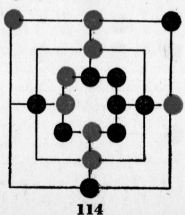

MILL

With the pieces all on the board, the second phase begins. Now, in turn, you move any man along a line to the adjacent intersection. If a mill is *opened* by moving a piece off the line, it counts as a new mill when it is *closed* again by moving the piece back. Your opponent's strategy of gaining a mill by force has left him no space to open his mill—a frequent result of this policy in laying down the pieces. Your policy will be to keep his mill jammed shut. For example, if he vacates 14 in order to play 13-14, you will block him by 15-14.

You commence with 1-10. He plays 14-21, and you duly block 15-14. He plays 23-24—ha, a mistake! Now you can make a mill on the line 1-10-22. With 20-23 you shut out interference. He now plays to minimize the consequences of his error. After he plays 21-20, and you move 2-1, he starts locking you up with 3-2. But you close the mill with 23-22 and remove 16, thus assuring that you can close a second mill by 17-16.

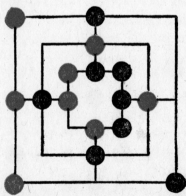

He plays 24-23, preventing you from opening your first mill. You play 17-16 and remove 23. He now has a tempo to open his mill, so he plays 18-17. Being one piece ahead

115

of him now, you force the play by 22-23. If he lets you close
this mill again, you will break up his, so he has to close at
once by 17-18. He removes 10. Now *you* have the tempo and
open by 16-17, also immobilizing his mill. You can use your
advantage to build up a second mill.

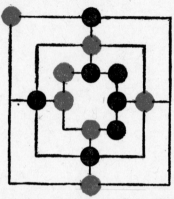

He tries 11-4, you play 1-10, he moves 2-3, and you intercept by 14-15. As you now have another mill coming on
22-23-24, he desperately opens with 13-14. You close with
17-16 and remove 18, smashing his mill. He plays 4-11, you
10-22, he 11-19, and he now threatens 14-21. But you get
there first with 15-24, remove 14, and he resigns. His game
is hopeless.

Laws of Mill: Each player commences with nine pieces.
One piece at a turn is placed upon any of the 24 *points* of
the board. When all pieces have been placed, play continues
by alternate *moves*. A piece may move to an adjacent vacant
point on the same line.

Whenever a player makes a *mill* by getting three of his
pieces on a line, he may remove any one adverse piece from
the board provided that it is not part of a mill. A mill may
be *opened* by moving a piece off the line; *closing* it by

MILL

moving the piece back counts as a separate mill, and entitles the player to remove another adverse piece.

The player first to be reduced to two pieces, or first to be unable to move in his turn, loses. (Some play that when a player is reduced to three pieces he may move "wild" from any point to any point, regardless of the lines.)

Pointers on Play: If White, playing first, takes one of the best points, as 5, Black can prevent the formation of a mill only by playing on an adjacent point, as 2, 4, 6 or 8. But more enterprising is to take another of the four key points, as 14, because White will lose by block if he immediately plays for a fork, thus:

WHITE	BLACK
5	14
8	2
7	9
12	16
11	10
4	6
19	

Whatever piece White removes, Black replaces, then White has to block at 21 and Black at 20. Now all of White's eight pieces are immobile, being held by Black's seven. Wherever White puts his last piece, Black can play adjacent and then run down this only free enemy.

Even if the player who forces an early mill does not run into a complete block, his extra piece by no means assures victory. In the example game, Black after becoming a piece up made a mistake and actually lost, but with the best of play he could no more than draw. Thus:

WHITE	BLACK
5	14
21	11
2	8
17	23
12	13
15	9
7	18 (7)
7	16
1	3
1-10	14-21
15-14	23-22
5-4!	8-5
7-8	etc.

White now maintains his pieces on 8, 14, 17, keeping the Black mill closed, and his other five pieces can meet all threats exerted by Black's six, without suffering paralysis. It seems as though the loss of a piece is an advantage to White in that it gives him elbow room to maneuver!

But it does not follow that a mill made by force in laying down the pieces is useless. On the contrary, it will usually bring victory if delayed just long enough so that the opponent runs out of pieces before he can blockade it. For example:

WHITE	BLACK
5	14
20	11
1	18
7	23?

Black's last move is a mistake. His policy of scattering his pieces to occupy many lines is correct—probably the game is intrinsically a draw if this policy is accurately carried out by both players—but here he should play 2 or 8 to intercept the White constellation. There follows:

WHITE	BLACK
6	4
19	21
8	2
9 (2)	2
15	13
7-12	any
12-7 (2)	

White wins as he now has two mills.

If each side makes one mill, the game is usually won by the first to open. The play is likely to be a matter of alternate captures, whence the name Mill (German Muhle, grinder)—the forces are ground down slowly but surely. But the player behind at the outset can sometimes overtake his opponent by collateral threats, especially the formation of a second mill. The ideal to be striven for is the *double-mill*, which grinds down the enemy in a hurry. For example, White pieces on 1, 2, 3, 4, 6. By moving 2-5 and 5-2, White closes a mill at each turn.

As has been remarked, the game is probably a draw with the best play on both sides. The drawing policy is to scatter the pieces so as to intercept on all possible lines. This is also the way to lure the opponent in traps, such as self-destruction through forcing the play too soon.

BACKGAMMON

Why You'll Like It: Backgammon is the oldest game of which we have record—equipment for playing it was found in an Egyptian tomb of 3000 B.C. To remain popular that long, a game *has* to be good.

What You Need: A backgammon board, complete with pieces. Two dice cups and four dice. A doubling cube.

The backgammon board is depicted in the illustration. The elongated triangles or *points,* as they are called, are colored alternately light and dark. Down the length of the board runs a *bar.*

The pieces or *stones* are in two colors, fifteen of each. We will call them black and white, and name the players accordingly, although the actual stones are usually colored black and red, or red and white.

The placement of the pieces on the board to commence a game is shown in the next illustration. Here the points are shown numbered, for convenience of reference.

BACKGAMMON

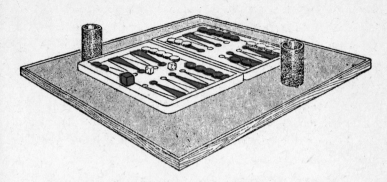

Backgammon Equipment: The board, stones, dice, dice cups, and doubling cube.

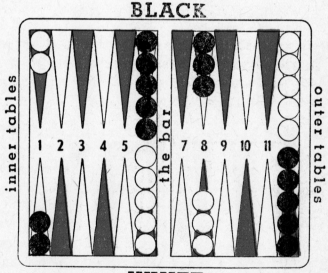

Terminology of the Board: Points on both sides are numbered from 1 to 12, inner table to outer. Each player moves his stones from 1 to 12 on the opponent's side of the board, and from 12 to 1 on his side.

Let's Play a Game: You decide by agreement who is to use the white stones and who the black; you take the white men for this game. To decide first turn, you each shake up one die in your dice cup and cast it. Your opponent, "Black," rolls a five and you roll a two. Having the higher number, he moves first, and for his first move he must use the numbers 5-2, which were thrown to decide first turn.

The moves consist in advancing stones from point to point in acordance with the numbers on the dice. There is no limit to the number of stones of one color that may stand on one point. But stones of different colors may never stand on the same point.

The direction in which you must move your stones is shown in the illustration. Your opponent moves in the contrary direction. The roll 5-2 is a rather undesirable opening roll. He plays it in the customary manner, by moving one stone from W12 (your 12-point) to B8 (his 8-point), and another from W12 to B11. Moves hereafter will be indicated as: W12-B8, W12-B11.

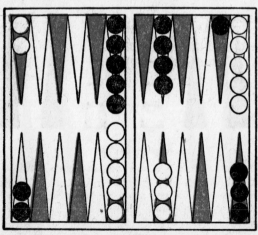

BACKGAMMON

In this move, he applied the 5 to one stone and the 2 to another. He could instead, had he wished, have applied both numbers to one stone, as by moving W12-B6.

What you are both trying to do is to get all your stones into your own inner or home table.

It is now your turn. You shake both your dice in your cup, and roll 6-1. This is a "natural," a desirable early roll, because it *makes the bar*. Your 7-point is your *bar point*. You move B12-W7 and W8-W7. Making a point is occupying it with two (or more) stones, because you thereby prevent any adverse stone from landing on that point. If you make your bar point early, you complete a barricade around the bar, your 6-, 7-, and 8-points, which makes it difficult for Black's *runners* (the two stones on your 1-point) to escape.

Now it is Black's turn. He shakes his two dice in his cup, casts them, and gets 3-2. With the 3 he *splits* his run-

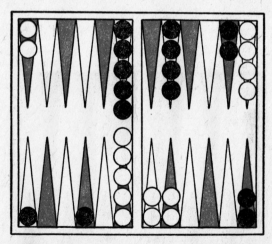

ners, advancing one of them B1-B4. With the 2 he *covers* his stone on B11, by bringing down another stone from his *comfort station,* your 12-point. Ordinarily it is not important to cover stones in the outer table, when the adverse runners are still far away (not split), but he has no preferable alternative to this move.

Your next roll is 2-2. In Backgammon, *doublets* are taken twice over. That means you may move four deuces, a total of eight points. You could move four different stones 2 points each, or one stone 8 points; or in any other arrangement you see fit. You start by moving two from W6-W4.

The Black single stone on your 4-point is a *blot.* If an adverse stone lands on a point ocupied by a blot, the latter is thereby *hit* and *sent to the bar.* You therefore pick up his stone on W-4 and place it literally on the bar. Hitting his blots is a method of delaying the opponent, so as to get ahead in the race to bring the stones around. You hit W4 with two stones so as to *make the point* and prevent his hitting back.

You still have two deuces to take. You decide to move the two stones from W7-W5. This opens your bar point, but

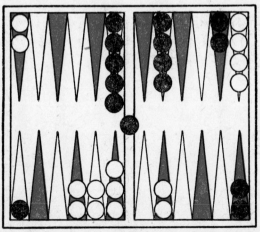

makes your 5-point. It is a good exchange when you have sent one of his men to the bar. As a general rule, the most important points to make are those in your home table, so long as the adverse runners have not escaped it.

Black now rolls 5-4. Having a stone on the bar, he may make no move until this stone enters. In effect, it is on an imaginary "zero" point just outside your home table, and must move from there to a higher point before any other move may be made. As you have *closed* your 5-point and 4-point, his roll of 5-4 does not permit his stone to enter. As he has *missed,* he picks up his dice without making a move.

You roll and get 5-4. There is a large choice how to take these numbers. You decide to move B12-W8 and B12-W9, *bringing down* two *builders*. Builders are stones in your outer table, useful for making points near your bar and in your home table. This is a conservative move, but if it permits you to make some more points in your home table you will have a decisive strategical advantage.

Black rolls 3-2—the first good roll he has had. He enters the man from the bar on your 3-point. Now, no longer having a man on the bar, he may use the rest of the roll. He uses the deuce to cover the man he has just entered, by W1-W3.

You roll 4-3. That 4 is just what you hoped for: You move B12-W9, making your 9-point. This point is particularly important as it is six away from his runners, which are now strongly barricaded. In fact, they can escape only by *combination* rolls, a 4 combined with another number higher than 2. For the 3 you bring down the last of your stones from your comfort station, B12-W10.

Black's next roll is 4-2. To split his runners would be suicidal, for you surely could hit the one remaining, and build a point in your home table at the same time. He takes the "natural" move, making his 4-point by B8-B4, B6-B4.

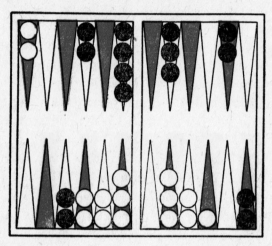

Before you make your next roll, you *double*. A *doubling cube* is furnished with most backgammon sets; on the faces of the cube are the numbers 2, 4, 8, 16, 32, 64. You indicate the double by turning the 2 up on the cube.

The double compels your opponent either to *drop*, concede loss of the game and lose a single game, or to *take*, play on for a double game. You have made this double because of the strong barricade you have established against his runners, while your own runners still find his board fairly open. Your opponent decides to accept the double, for he reckons that the odds against his winning are no worse than 3 to 1, and in such a case a double should be accepted. Your runners have a long way to go to reach home, and the Black stones have good prospects of hitting them.

BACKGAMMON

Your roll proves to be 3-2. Almost, but not quite, what you wanted! With 3-1 you could have made your 7-point and completed a prime. A *prime* is a formation of twelve stones occupying six consecutive points. Enemy runners trapped back of a prime of course cannot escape, because 6, the highest number, will not carry them beyond it.

You decide to "shoot the works" by moving W10-W7, leaving the blot there within reach of his runners. If you get an ace before he gets a 4 you can cover by the extra man on your 8-point. For the 2, you split your runners, B1-B3.

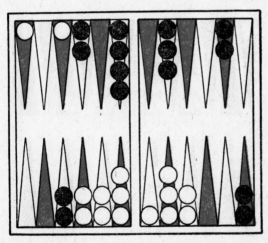

Black hopes to roll a 4, but gets 3-1. Although the total is 4, he cannot use it to hit the blot on your bar point. To use the total roll with one stone, he must find an appropriate intermediate point open. Since he cannot move W3-W6 nor W3-W4, he cannot hit.

He might make his 5-point, but is afraid that your runner on B3 will skip lightly over his bar and escape. In desperation he plays B6-B3, hitting, and B8-B7. The idea of this move is that if you hit back in re-entering, he may get some more runners into your home board—and against a prime or near-prime three or four runners can usually fight better than only two. If you do not hit in re-entering, he may be able to make up his board quickly and force you to break your prime by immobilizing your runners. The rule is, that if able to use your rolls in any way you must do so.

You now have a stone on the bar. You roll 5-1. Hooray! You enter the stone on B5, then move W8-W7, completing the prime.

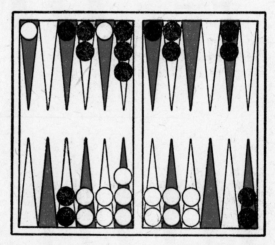

Now let's turn to the last stage of the game. You have succeeded in getting your runners out at last, though you were hit many times in the process; and now you reach the position of the illustration on the next page.

It is your turn. You roll 5-1 and move W7-W2, W7-W6. Black rolls 6-2 and moves W3-W11. Your next roll is 4-1.

Now that all your fifteen stones are inside your home board, you may begin to *bear off*. You continue to move

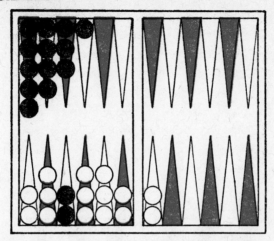

your men in the same direction, toward the imaginary "zero" point just outside your 1-point. Thus you move them off the board, and once off they stay off. The player who first *bears off* all his stones in this manner wins the game.

To play the 4-1 you simply remove one stone each from your 4-point and 1-point. Black rolls 3-2 and moves W11-B9.

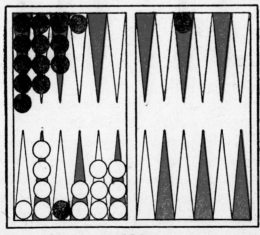

Your next roll is 5-5. You remove the three stones from your 5-point and move one stone W6-W1. It is not compulsory to bear off in preference to *moving down*. You could have played the three stones from W6 to W1, then removing only one stone from the 5-point. This move would be preferred if your opponent had a closed board. But in the present position you are not worried about being hit; you will probably be able to re-enter. So you try to bear off your men as fast as possible.

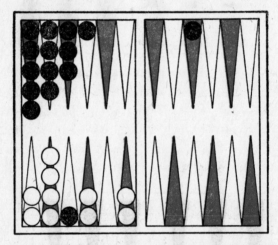

Black rolls 3-3, and his remaining runner still cannot escape. He moves B9-B3 and B4-B1. That uses three 3's; as he cannot move any other stone three points, he loses the fourth 3.

Now you get the same roll 3-3, and remove the two men from your 6-point. You also pick up the blot from your board and put it on the bar, for your move necessarily hits the Black stone. Black has the misfortune to roll 2-2 and his stone cannot enter.

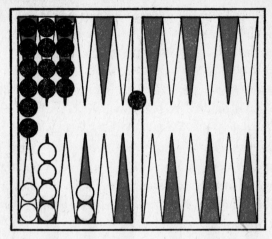

Your roll of 6-4 takes the two stones off your 4-point. (The 6 may be applied to the 4-point because you have no stones left on the 6- and 5-points.) Black rolls 5-4, so his stone enters and advances to W9. With 4-1 you then bear off a stone from the 1-point and another from the 2-point (for the 4, all higher points being bare). Again Black has

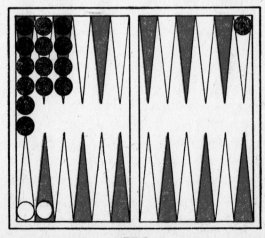

tough luck, rolling 1-1 and so getting his runner only to B12. You roll 6-2, and after taking two men off the 2-point have only two stones left in the board.

Black needs a 6 to bear off a man, but rolls 5-3 and so concedes *gammon*. Any roll you make is bound to bear off your last two stones. He is gammoned because you have borne off your last man before he has borne off a single man. Gammon doubles the loss, and as the game was already doubled (by you), you win four points for the game.

Laws of Backgammon: *First turn.* Each player rolls one die, and higher has first turn. If equal numbers are cast, the game is automatically doubled, and the players cast again until unlike numbers are rolled. (The number of automatic doubles allowed should be limited by agreement.) The player having the first turn uses the numbers cast in determining the turn as his first roll. (It may be agreed that the first player will cast both his dice again for his first roll.)

Moves. The player must if possible use both numbers of his cast, applying them separately to two (or more) stones or both to one stone. In the latter case, the stone must find intermediate points open so as to be able to use the numbers separately.

A move consists in advancing a stone a number of points corresponding to the number on the die. A stone may not come to rest on a point occupied by two or more adverse stones. Any number of stones of the same color may rest on one point.

Doublets (like numbers on both dice) are taken twice over, e.g., 5-5 is taken as four 5s, a total of 20 points. The numbers may be applied to one, two, three or four stones.

BACKGAMMON

The player must use all of his roll that he can. If able to use only one of two unlike numbers, he must use the higher if possible.

Blots. A single stone on a point is a *blot*. If an adverse stone comes to rest on that point, the blot is picked up and placed *on the bar*. Before he may make any other move, the owner must *enter* the blot in the adverse inner table. A point is *open* if it is not occupied by two or more adverse stones; a blot must enter upon an open point of the adverse inner table by the cast of that number on one die. (E. g., if only the 5-point is open, a 5 must be cast on one die for entry— a total of 5 on the two dice, as 3-2, may not be used.) If unable to enter a stone from the bar, the player passes his turn; if the adverse inner table is entirely closed, the player does not roll at all.

Bearing off. A player may *bear off* whenever all his stones remaining on the board lie within his own inner table. To bear off a stone is to remove it from the board, by the cast of a number corresponding to the point on which it rests, either on one die or both together. (E. g., a stone on the 4-point may be borne off on cast of any 4, or 3-1, 2-2.) Having choice, a player may move within the inner table in preference to bearing off.

A number cast on one die which is higher than or equal to the outermost point on which the player has any stone must be applied to that point, and a stone must be borne off. (E. g., if the player has two stones on his 1-point and one on his 5-point, the roll of 6-1 compels removal of the latter, but it is permissible to move it first to the 4-point to use the 1, should the player not wish to bear a stone off the 1-point.) If, in bearing off, a player leaves a blot, and it is hit, he must enter this stone and bring it around to his inner table before he can resume bearing off.

The first player to bear off all fifteen stones wins the game.

If the loser has borne off no stone, he is *gammoned* and loses double. If, besides having borne off no stone, he has a stone left in the adverse inner table or on the bar, he is *backgammoned* and loses treble.

Doubling. Either player may be the first to propose a double. Thereafter the right to double alternates. A double may be proposed only in the player's turn to roll, before he rolls. If it is accepted, play continues with the current value of the game doubled. If it is refused, the opponent of the doubler loses the game at its current value, and the game is abandoned. The basic value may also be increased by automatic doubles, if agreed (see *First Turn*) and by gammon and backgammon (see *Bearing off*).

Irregularities: If at any time it is discovered that the stones were wrongly placed for commencement of play, the game is void.

The dice must be cast, and both must land, in the table at the player's right. If either die lands elsewhere or is *cocked* (not flat on the board), both dice must be picked up and cast again.

The player must leave his dice on the board until his play is completed. Should he pick them up before that time, his opponent may either void the play or require any partial play to be retracted and the offender to cast again.

If the player moves a stone from its position, except for the stated purpose of arranging, it must if possible be played. A move once made may not be retracted. (Instead of this rigid rule, most people prefer to play that no move is final until the player has picked up his dice.)

If a move is made that is illegal or does not correspond with the dice, it must be retracted on demand of the opponent if made before he has rolled. Thereafter, an incorrect move may be rectified only by agreement.

A cast of the dice made before the opponent has completed his play is void.

Pointers on Play: *Opening moves.* The most desirable opening rolls are the "naturals" which make points: 6-1, 3-1, 4-2. While 5-3 makes the 3-point, this point is of much less value than the points nearer the bar. Making the 2-point with a 6-4 is considered a very poor play. All rolls other than naturals give choice of play, in which the objectives to be selected from are (a) to bring down *builders* from the "comfort station" (adverse 12-point) into the outer table, whence they will assist in making points near the bar; (b) to start the runners on their way; (c) to offer a "gambit" by laying a blot on the 5-point or the bar point, hoping to cover it next turn.

The following tabulations show the possible ways of playing the opening rolls that have been recommended. The first alternative in each case is that preferred by Edmond Hoyle. (Backgammon is one of the very few games in which "according to Hoyle" still has any meaning.)

Hoyle's prescription for the poor rolls is generally to split the runners. The modern tendency is to concentrate on building a blockade against the adverse runners, bringing down builders and blotting freely so long as the adverse home table is still wide open. But the classic moves still have many advocates.

135

The moves are given for White as the first player.

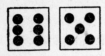

Take B1-B12 ("Lover's Leap"), getting one runner to safety. No good alternative.

Move B1-B11; or B12-W7 and B1-B5. The first is the conservative move; the odds are 25:11 that the opponent cannot hit the blot. The second is a gambit; the blot on the bar is easily hit, but White may make the adverse 5-point in compensation.

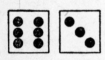

Move B1-B10, or B12-W7 and B1-B4. Same considerations as for 6-4, but 6-3 is not so good a roll for either purpose.

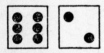

Move B12-W5; or B12-W7 and B12-W11. A gambit either way, trying to make the 5-point or the bar.

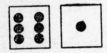

A natural. Move B12-W7 and W8-W7, making the bar point.

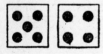

Move B1-B10, or B12-W8 and B1-B4. A succession of 5's at the outset of the game is very awkward. The first alternative avoids loading up the 8-point. The second has the merit of trying for a good point.

A natural, if you want to play it that way. Move W8-W3 and W6-W3. Some players prefer to move B12-W8 and B12-W10, bringing down a builder.

Move B12-W8 and B12-W11. One of the worst rolls.

Move B12-W8 and W6-W5; or B12-W8 and B1-B2. As to the second, there are schools of "splitters" and "non-splitters," the issue being whether the runners are better off on the 1-point or divided.

Move B12-W9 and B12-W10; or B1-B5 and B12-W10. The first goes in for building in a big way. The second puts two irons in the fire.

A natural. Move W8-W4 and W6-W4, making the 4-point.

Move B12-W9 and W6-W5; or B12-W9 and B1-B2. The first has the same object as the gambit play of 6-2, but with distinctly better prospects. The second is the "splitter" school recommendation.

Move B12-W10 and B12-W11; or B1-B4 and B12-W11. Same ideas as 4-3.

A natural. Move W8-W5 and W6-W5, making the 5-point. Viewed by some as the best non-doublet roll.

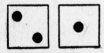

Move B12-W11 and W6-W5; or B12-W10. The second is for timid souls who shrink from the classical gambit.

Where it is agreed that the first player is to roll both dice, the first cast may be a doublet. The following is "the book" on opening doublets—also applicable to any early doublet if the move is possible and nothing better offers. In each case, two men are moved together.

 Move B1-B7 and B12-W7, making both bar points. Many a quick double has been made on the strength of this roll— but if you get another it will be mighty awkward.

 Move B12-W3. As with 6-6, one 5-5 gives you a nice lead, but a second is a headache.

 It is said that "there is no wrong way to play 4-4." The classical school gives prime importance to the 5-point, and so moves B12-W5. A frequent alternative is B12-W9 and B1-B5, taking the adverse 5-point and making a good outer point. Even B1-B9 has its advocates.

 Most-played is W8-W5 and W6-W3, making the 5-point and 3-point. An alternative is B12-W7, making the bar point. Hoyle gives the alternative W8-W5 and B1-B4, but this is seldom seen in modern play.

 Move W6-W4 and B12-W11; or move B1-B5. Hoyle's alternative of W6-W4 and B1-B3 has been relegated to limbo.

BACKGAMMON

 The tops—more prized than even 6-6. Move W6-W5 and W8-W7, making both the key points, the 5 and the bar.

Early play. If there were no hitting, the game would reduce to the luck of the rolls. The battle centers around the blots—the effort to avoid blotting, to hit adverse blots, to keep adverse men on the bar. The foremost objective of early play is then to make points in one's own home table or near the bar. The ideal of course is the establishment of a *prime,* with one or more enemy stones trapped behind it. Making points on one's side of the board not only impedes the immediate exit of the adverse runners, but—and this is usually more important—tends to set up a lasting strategic advantage. The more complete the blockade, the fewer chances can the opponent afford to take in blotting, so long as you have any runners behind his men. As a rule it is the late hit, not the early hit, that brings victory.

With some indifferent opening rolls, blots are laid on the 5-point or the bar point, because the consequences of being hit are not likely to be serious. The loss of time in having to enter a man from the bar and bring him around again is often compensated by the fact that he fights back on his journey. And at the beginning of the game, when the opponent holds only his 6-point, entry is usually immediate.

But let a player make two more points in his board, or the bar and one inner point, and his opponent takes great risk in trying any such gambits. The added points mean more than added difficulty of entering; they give added positions of safety for builders. The adverse board may be further closed, even to a complete *shut-out,* very rapidly.

It is a mistake (according to the modern view) to use the runners to absorb awkward early rolls. At home on the enemy 1-point, the runners are a potential threat that becomes more acute as one's own board is built up. Without some fighters back of the enemy, the shut-out has no meaning. The modern practice is not to split the runners except to take them to the outer table with good prospects of escape. If they cannot come out on doublets, take them out one at a time, leaving the rearmost on the 1-point until the foremost has reached the comfort station. Thus, on 6-4 or 5-4 the leap of one runner to the 11-point or 10-point is reasonable, because the opponent has to roll a 2 or a 3 to hit (from his comfort station). But to carry one man to the 9-point, or to advance both a little way, is dubious. Worst of all is to advance a runner to the adverse bar point on a 6 and leave him there, and the error can be compounded by advancing the other runner within the inner table. Such a misbegotten "gambit" deserves to see both runners hit and the adverse home table made up in short order.

If a roll gives opportunity to get one runner or both into safety, it may well be taken—for the reason that the roll is necessarily a high one, so that the player is willing to forego hits and play a pure *running* game. But mark that the adverse bar is an unhealthy point to make. There is no alternative but to advance the runners there on an early 6-6, but as a rule they should not be allowed to linger. The opponent can make up his board unimpeded, and if one runner has to be left on the 7-point while the other leaps to safety, it is the easiest blot to hit. The adverse comfort station is 6 points away, and 6 has the highest probability of any number in the dice.

BACKGAMMON

The forward game. The stage of play in which no more hits are possible, all pieces being past the enemy, is called the *running* game. Here the outcome is decided solely by the higher rolls—and the head start. The object of the *forward game,* as it is called, is to reach the running stage with a head start, gained by avoiding any excessive delay and by delaying the opponent so far as practicable. It does not necessarily mean bringing out the runners early, but it does mean trying to get them out safely once and for all when they do emerge.

The forward game is the natural choice when the rolls permit. It is also the policy of the player who is behind in the race, if he is not too far behind, for he may catch up with a few high rolls. But if he is *very* far behind, and especially if two or more of his runners are trapped behind a blockade that would prevent his using high doublets even if he rolled them, this player has to consider switching to a *back game.*

The back game. This is the policy of accepting—nay, forcing—a very great delay, in the expectation of regaining all the lost ground and more at a later stage. The back game player holds several points in the adverse inner table, having had a number of blots hit. The opponent, being ahead in time, is trying to get his forces into his home table at the time the other is forming a near-prime in his outer table. For lack of opposition, the blockade can be constructed easily; meanwhile the opponent is having to stack fifteen men on three or four points (perhaps less) open to him in his own board. The dice may force him to blot, and a blot once hit may be held in by the prime while the back player gets all his runners out and around.

The back game is subject to many ills. It may reach an ideal position and then be ruined by bad rolls, such as high doublets that break up a prime. The runners left in the adverse home table may succeed in hitting, but then may have such difficulty in emerging that the prime is broken first. As the runners leave, the opponent may be able to move down in his board, making the points vacated, and a counter-hit may be ruinous. The inexpert player is likely to add to these inherent woes by attempting a back game with insufficient means. To have real prospects of a hit, it is usually necessary to hold at least three points in the adverse board. That takes six stones at least, leaving insufficient for a complete prime. The blockade with which it is hoped to restrain the adverse blot—when and if hit—is thus best-placed in the adverse outer table, where it can quickest be enlarged by the emerging runners. But then it has to be *walked* around the board and into the home table. *Walking a prime* is an art in itself. As shown in the diagram, white takes the first opportunity to place a single stone on

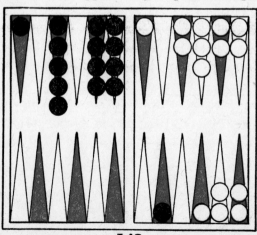

the point ahead of his prime. He will cover the blot only with one of the two extra stones, or by a stone from the rear end of the prime.

When the back player has got what he wants, the question sometimes arises whether to hit every blot in sight, for the opponent may be forced to blot repeatedly in his home table. Generally speaking, the safest course is to hit *only one* blot and hold that to the bitter end by a walking prime. The danger of hitting two or more blots is that they may make a point in the outer table, the prime being compelled to walk past.

Running and bearing off. In a pure running game, do not waste points. That means, get your men into the home board as fast as possible—don't worry about the fact that you have most of them stacked on the 6-point. Use the dice to get a stone from the adverse outer table *precisely* to your 12-point, and from your own outer table *precisely* to your 6-point. With choice of moves fulfilling this condition—or where you cannot get a stone to either the 12 or the 6—move the stone farthest from home.

In bearing off, as a rule take off as many stones as possible at each turn, regardless of the looks of your board. Don't move down when you can bear off. Exception arises in the last stage when you can calculate directly that it is better to move down. Example: You have three stones on your 1-point, two on your five. Your opponent has two stones each on his 1- and 2-points. You roll 5-1. Off comes a stone from the 5-point, but don't bear off from the 1-point. Move 5-4. Your only chance to win is to throw a doublet next turn, and if you leave the stone on the 5 you will need 6-6 or 5-5. By moving down you also allow 4-4 to get you off.

LIAR DICE

Why You'll Like It: This is the favorite game of officers' clubs in the United States Army, and for good reason, because it combines elements of chance, skill and psychology. It is not necessarily the best hand that wins in Liar Dice, but the player who convinces the other that his hand is best. The game is like Poker in that respect, but moves faster and gives even more opportunity for a good bluff to win over a better hand.

What You Need: Ten dice, two dice cups, and a light screen. Two wooden panels fastened together in an inverted V make the ideal screen. It should be about nine inches high and a foot long. In lieu of a specially-made screen, a large thin book such as an atlas, standing half-opened on the table, will do.

LIAR DICE

Let's Play a Game: You and I each take five dice and one cup, and we set up the screen between us on the table. The dice are to be shaken up in the cup and rolled so that they bounce against the screen, which also conceals our rolls from each other.

First we must determine who is to be the first *caller*. We each cast one die. You roll a six and I roll an ace. That makes me the caller, as the ace ranks higher than the six.

Now we begin. We each roll all five dice simultaneously out of the cup. Our primary object is to make the best possible "poker hand" of five dice. The possible poker hands rank as follows:

> Five of a kind, as 1-1-1-1-1, the highest hand
> Four of a kind, as 2-2-2-2-5
> Full house, a triplet and a pair, as 3-3-3-6-6
> High straight, 6-5-4-3-2
> Low straight, 5-4-3-2-1
> Triplet, as 4-4-4-1-2
> Two pairs, as 6-6-3-3-2
> One pair, as 4-4-6-3-1
> High spot, as 1-6-4-3-2
> The rank of the dice is: 1 (high), 6, 5, 4, 3, 2. Ties between hands of the same class are broken by the rank of the dice.

As caller, I must announce my hand. I have rolled:

"Fives and deuces and a three," I say. Of course I mean 5-5-2-2-3. I might simply have said "fives up" in Poker fashion, but you are entitled to know every spot, so I save time by telling you at once.

You look at your hand, which is:

You announce:

"No good. I have three fours, a five and an ace" (4-4-4-5-1).

Now, that's a lie! You don't have three of a kind. But the whole point of Liar Dice is that you may announce any hand you wish, regardless of what you actually have!

"That beats me," say I. I think it is likely that you actually have three fours, so I intend to roll again and try for a better hand. I pick up some of my dice, shake them in the cup and roll them again. You listen carefully, for you may tell by the sound how many dice I have picked up, and sometimes this will provide you a clue to what I actually may have.

Your ear tells you that I rolled three dice, so you know that I saved a pair. On taking my second roll, I can leave as many of the dice standing from my first roll as I wish, and roll only the others. You decide that maybe I had two pairs and saved the fives; maybe I had only one pair to begin with.

After my second roll, I announce:

"I got my third five. Also a four and a deuce" (5-5-5-4-2).

The cardinal rule of the game is that on every announcement you must either claim a higher hand than your opponent has announced or else "call him a liar," lift the screen and see if he actually has what he claimed. I might have claimed 4-4-4-6-1, which would have just topped your claim of 4-4-4-5-1. But if I had (inadvertently) announced any lower hand I would have lost the game at once.

It is now your turn to announce, and you in turn are bound to put in a higher claim than mine, or else lift the screen. If you decide to claim a higher hand, you can defer doing so until you have rolled again, if you wish. You decide to carry on your bluff of having three of a kind. So you save the 6-4-4 from your first roll, and cast the other two dice again. You get a pair of 3's. Now your hand is:

But you announce:
"I caught the fourth four and a three" (4-4-4-4-3).

I mull that over a bit, but decide that you may actually have four of a kind. So I roll two dice and get this:

At this point I *must* announce a higher hand than you last claimed (which was 4-4-4-4-3). Before I rolled again, I could have lifted the screen, or I could have simply announced a higher hand than yours without rolling. But once I rolled, I committed myself to beating your announced hand, and I have to say I have beaten it even if it makes me a "liar."

So now I announce:

"Four fives and an ace" **(5-5-5-5-1)**.

That is so much higher than any hand you can hope to make in one roll (we each may take three rolls altogether) that you decide not to try to top it. You lift the screen and look at what I actually have. In effect, this says "I think you're a liar!"

When you lift the screen after my announcement, you lose the game if my hand is as good as or better than I claimed. You win if it is not so good. In this case, since I actually have 5-5-5-6-3, but I announced that I had 5-5-5-5-1, you win the game.

You replace the screen and we start the next game. You are now the caller, as you won the previous game. Since the play moves fast, it is usual to play two games out of three or three out of five.

Laws of Liar Dice: *The hands.* The various hands rank as follows, high to low:

Five of a kind, as 1-1-1-1-1, the highest hand
Four of a kind, as 2-2-2-2-5
Full house, a triplet and a pair, as 3-3-3-6-6
High straight, 6-5-4-3-2
Low straight, 5-4-3-2-1
Triplet, as 4-4-4-1-2
Two pairs, as 6-6-3-3-2
One pair, as 4-4-6-3-1
High spot, as 1-6-4-3-2

The numbers rank, high to low: 1, 6, 5, 4, 3, 2, except that 1 ranks below 2 in making a straight.

As between two hands of the same class, the higher hand is that with the higher group of five, four or three of a kind;

LIAR DICE

the highest pair of two-pair hands, or the higher second pair if the highest pairs are the same; the higher pair in one-pair hands; and the highest outside spot if the groups are tied. Thus, 1-1-1-1-1 beats 6-6-6-6-6; 4-4-4-4-5 beats 3-3-3-3-6 or 4-4-4-4-3; 5-5-5-2-2 beats 4-4-4-6-6; 3-3-2-2-1 beats 3-3-2-2-4; 1-1-4-3-2 beats 5-5-1-6-4.

Announcements: The caller first announces his hand, after the first roll. (In some circles, it is customary for the caller first to state that he is satisfied with his roll or propose that both players roll again.)

Thereafter each player in turn must either announce a higher hand than was claimed by his opponent, or lift the screen. If a player announces an equal or lower hand, he loses the game at once.

Lifting the screen ends the game. If the opponent of the lifter has as good a hand as he claimed, he wins; if he has a lower hand, he loses.

Each player is entitled to three rolls per game. For his second or third rolls he may save as many of the dice from his previous rolls as he wishes. The dice saved should be pushed toward one end of the screen and the remaining dice rolled against the other end.

When a player elects to take his second or third roll, in lieu of announcing a better hand, he stands committed to do so: he may not then lift the screen until he has announced and his opponent has again announced. A player may use both his rolls after the first before making an announcement, if he wishes.

An announcement should specify the spots on all five dice. If a player makes an incomplete announcement, as by saying "I have a pair of aces," he must on demand complete it.

Pointers on Play: Liar Dice is very much a matter of playing your particular opponent. But some general principles can be laid down.

The worst hand to try to improve is a straight. If you get one on your first roll, announce it correctly, stand on it, and lift the screen if your opponent claims higher.

If you make a full house or better, announce it correctly and back it to be good.

Overclaims are thus mainly confined to hands from two pairs to full house. But if you do not overdo it, you can occasionally build up a bluff that you have made four of a kind, even when you haven't. This bluff must usually start with a convincing demonstration that you have three of a kind, by rolling only two dice after your first roll.

The biggest winner is the mild bluff that eggs your opponent into an overclaim. Here you must remember to leave him something to roll for. If you overclaim on three of a kind, a full house, or four of a kind, make the spots low enough so that he has a fair chance to roll for a higher hand of the same kind. Once he decides to roll, he can no longer hook your bluff.

If you play often with the same opponent, "it pays to advertise." Make some bluffs even though you are very likely to be exposed, for then he will always be suspicious of you and you will sometimes hook him when you have the middling hand you claim—he lifts the screen and so loses the chance to outroll you.

SNIFF

Why You'll Like It: Like other dominoes games, Sniff is so simple that children can play it almost before they learn to count, but unlike many dominoes games, it permits the exercise of skill to a considerable extent. The French, who love to linger at tables of their sidewalk cafe and play dominoes while they sip their *aperitifs*, have employed the principle of Sniff for many years; so have the English, who call the game (in an earlier form) Muggins. In some fine American clubs, neither Gin Rummy nor any other card game, including even Bridge, can compete with Sniff for popularity.

What You Need: A set of dominoes, up to double-six, and pencil and paper for scoring.

Let's Play a Game: First turn all 28 dominoes face down on the table and shuffle them. You and your opponent should both do some mixing, so as to decrease the chance

151

of keeping track of the position of any domino—consciously or unconsciously.

Now draw seven dominoes at random. Stand them on edge, facing you—and be careful not to jiggle the table! You find that your hand is:

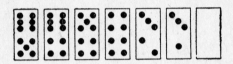

The next step is to determine who shall play first. Each of you draws one extra bone from the boneyard. (Dominoes are commonly called bones, and the boneyard is the balance of the set after you have drawn your seven bones each.) You get the 6-0 and he shows the 4-1. As your bone is the "heavier" (has a higher total count), you have first turn. Now the 6-0 and 4-1 have to be shuffled back into the boneyard. (This is the usual way of deciding first turn. If you want to avoid the extra shuffling, flip a coin instead.)

For your first play, you lay the 6-4 on the table. The reason for choosing this bone is that the two ends total 10 points. Whenever you make the total of the open ends of the layout 5, 10, 15 or any other multiple of 5, you score that amount.

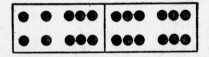

Your opening play of the 6-4 compels your opponent to lay down a bone with either a 6 or a 4 at one end. He puts the 6-6 endwise against the 6-4, and since the two open ends still total 10, he also scores 10 points.

The 6-6, and all others with the same number on both ends, are called doublets. The first doublet to be played in a game becomes *sniff*, and is open four ways, that is, a bone may be played on each of the four sides. Your opponent was entitled to play the 6-6 endwise because it is sniff. All other doublets have to be placed crosswise, so that both ends count. Had he placed the 6-6 crosswise, the total of the open ends would have been 16, scoring nothing.

You are fortunate in having the 6-5, because you can now play it off the side of sniff to score 15.

Your opponent comes right back at you with the 5-0, which makes a score of 10. But by adding 0-0 you keep the count the same and likewise score 10.

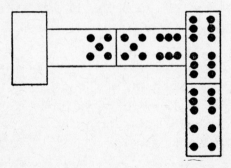

His next play is the 2-0, which makes the open ends total 12. You cannot score either, so you take the opportunity to get rid of your other doublet, the 4-4. Remember that this has to go crosswise, so the open ends total 16. Although both ends of the 4-4 are counted, it does not divide that branch of the layout into two open ends. Only one 4-bone can be played on the 4-4, after which the 4-4 is no longer open.

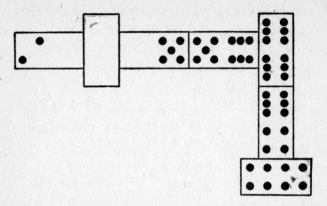

Your opponent lays down the 4-2. He could play this either on the 4-4 or on the 2-0. He chooses the latter, probably in hope that you are running out of 4s. But you disappoint him by producing the 5-4, which you are careful to play on the doublet so as to score 15. Played on the single 4, it would make the total 19.

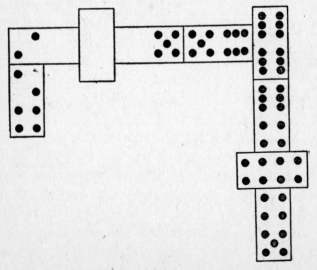

SNIFF

He plays the 4-3, making the count 14. You add the 3-2, reducing the count to 13. He plays the 6-2 off the other side of sniff, thus sprouting the fourth open end from it and scoring 15.

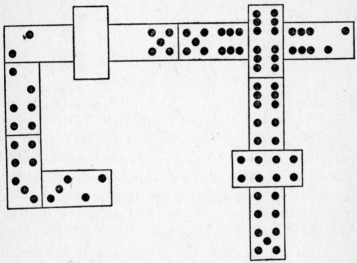

You have one bone left in your hand, the 3-1. The layout calls for 6, 5 or 2. As you cannot play, you must draw from the boneyard until you get one of these numbers. On your very first draw you luckily get the 6-1. This was just the bone you wanted. It gives you a score of 10.

Now your opponent draws from the boneyard. He is evidently lacking 5, 2 and 1. His first draw is the 5-2. He could play it on either of two ends. Cannily he puts it on the 5— had he played it on the 2, you would have scored 15 in your last turn. But you get rid of the 3-1 anyhow, and then you are "out."

You score whatever your opponent has left in his hand when you go out. His remaining bone is the 4-0, so you score

5—the count of the loser's hand is taken to the nearest multiple of 5. Altogether you have scored 65 points while he has made only 35. You have a good start toward the game, which is 200.

Laws of Sniff: *Drawing.* Each player draws seven bones for his hand. If unable to play in turn, a player must draw from the boneyard until able. It is permissible to draw even though able to play. If unable to play after the boneyard is exhausted, a player passes his turn.

First turn is decided by lot, as by drawing extra bones; the heavier plays first. But after the first deal of a game, the winner of one deal plays first in the next.

Sniff. The first play may be any bone. The first doublet played is sniff, and is open four ways. It, therefore, may be placed endwise or crosswise. All other doublets must be placed crosswise.

Scoring. Whenever a player makes the total of the open ends a multiple of 5 he scores that amount. In counting open ends: An *end* of sniff always counts (or the end of a branch built upon it) ; a *side* of sniff counts only after the first bone has been played off it; both ends of a non-sniff doublet on an open end count.

Going out. The first to go out by getting rid of his hand wins the deal. The winner scores the total of points left in the loser's hand, taken to the nearest 5. If the game ends in a block, with neither able to play and the boneyard exhausted, the lighter hand wins the difference of the hands, taken to the nearest 5.

Game. The first to reach 200 wins a game. If 200 is reached by scores made during play, the deal is not played out.

SNIFF

Muggins (optional). If a player makes the total of open ends a multiple of 5 and fails to claim the score, his opponent may claim it and score it. When one player alone keeps score on paper, he must announce orally each score he claims: the act of writing the score in his column, without oral notice, does not protect him from muggins.

Irregularities: If in drawing for first play a player exposes more than one bone, he is deemed to have drawn the lightest.

If a player draws too many bones for his hand, he must keep them all. If he draws too few, his opponent may demand that he draw as many more as are required to bring his hand to the proper number; but the opponent may not so demand after he has played.

If a player exposes a bone in drawing from the boneyard, he must take it. If a bone in the boneyard is exposed in any other way, the boneyard is reshuffled.

If a player announces and scores more points than he is entitled to, his opponent may demand correction before next playing; after that, the erroneous score stands. (Either player may so demand correction when too few points are scored, unless muggins is being played.)

Pointers on Play: The example game shows more scoring in play than occurs in the average deal. The average expectation is to make 20 to 30 points in play. Yet it remains true that the game is won primarily by these scores; the points made by going out first are relatively unimportant.

This fact has two applications: (a) score whenever you can; (b) play to increase the chance of scoring rather than the chance of going out.

The advice to "score whenever you can" would seem to be superfluous. But it has to be given if only to indicate the exceptions. Once in a while a player has to draw most of the boneyard. If this happens to your opponent, and you have only a few bones left, naturally you should concentrate upon going out. For example, suppose you are left with the 5-3 and 6-0. The open ends of the layout are 6, 5, 4, 3. By playing the 5-3 on the 3 you can score 20. But then if your opponent plays on the 6, you are blocked. By foregoing the score of 20, and playing the 6-0 first, you are sure to go out next turn.

In passing, let's give advice to your opponent in this predicament. If stuck with most of the boneyard, concentrate on scoring *each turn,* if there is an unplayed bone that will make a score. For this purpose, dig as deep as you have to, and if your opponent has only one or two bones left, take the whole boneyard. You will then know exactly what his bones are. Sometimes the knowledge is no help, for he can go out whatever you do. But more often you will see exactly how to keep him blocked until you have unloaded a great deal. At worst, you can almost surely score enough in play to more than compensate for any extra bones you had to draw.

Here is another aside on blocking play. With four ends open, it is rarely possible to play so as to *force* your opponent to draw many bones. But the possibility may arise if the boneyard has been depleted (as by voluntary drawing for particular scoring bones). The way to block is to make two, three, or all the open ends the same, particularly in a number of which you hold the "case" bones (the only ones left of their suit). There are eight *ends* in each suit, two of which are on the doublet. If all four open ends show the same number, the doublet alone may be a "case," or two other bones may be cases. When the doublet is a case, its play will block the game entirely.

Now back to our muttons. The blocks and near-blocks of which we have been speaking are the exception. The rule is that little drawing is necessary if you concentrate on going out in a hurry. But then you will often have to give up scoring chances. As a rule, score whenever you can, and let the going out take care of itself.

The principle (b) is just an extension of principle (a). If you were to think only of going out, whenever choice offered you would play so as to leave yourself the greatest possible assortment of different numbers. For example, suppose you are left with 6-3, 6-1, 3-1, 5-4 and the layout calls for 6, 5, 4 or 2. You cannot score. The natural choice of play seems to be the 6-1, for then you are sure of being able to play next turn, and are left with 6, 5, 4, 3, 1. Yet (with no special reasons to the contrary showing in the layout) the better choice is the 5-4. This leaves you without 5s or 4s, and you will have to draw if your opponent adds 6-0 or 6-2 to the 6-end—yet all these risks are worth taking to save the 6-1.

To see why this is, you should first play several games of Sniff. You will observe that a player who has just scored has a good chance of scoring again in his next turn. There is usually some bone that will *complement* the bone next played by his opponent. If this complementary bone is not already in the layout, and if the scoring player does not hold it in his hand, he often does well to dig in the boneyard for it. The fact that your opponent has just scored thus puts you on the defensive, and the best defense of all is to make a score yourself, switching the sequence.

Certain bones are of intrinsic value, because they almost always score after a score. (Exercise your imagination by digging out the exceptions for yourself.)

The first class of these "naturals" is: 5-5, 5-0, 0-0, 6-1. Normally each of these adds or subtracts 5 or 0 to the count of ends.

The second class is the two bones having 5 and 0 on one end, with the number of the sniff doublet on the other. For example, if sniff is 3-3, 5-3 and 3-0 are valuable because if played off a side of sniff they add 5 or 0 to the count. Of course these "naturals" lose their value after both sides of sniff have sprouted.

The third class is 6-4, 4-1 and 3-2, which score as the opening play.

The fourth class is 6-3, 4-2, 2-1, any of which played on a doublet of its lower number leaves the total of open ends unchanged. These are ranked low simply because the opportunity to utilize their virtues is comparatively rare.

Principle (b) means that you should keep any naturals of the first and second class until they can be used for scoring, even at the cost of stripping the hand of other numbers. Digging three or four deep in the boneyard for a specific bone that will let you score has the added chance of gathering a natural or two besides.

With experience, you can carry the principle further and *build toward* scores by calculating how the play may go, in view of your hand and the inferences you make as to what your opponent may hold. As a starter, practice calculating what chances your opponent has to score after each of your possible plays. Opportunities for accurate defense often bob up. An example is your opponent's last play in the example game. At this juncture, he drew 5-2 and could play on either of two ends. He knew you had just drawn, being out of 6, 5, 2. If you could go out after his play of 5-2, it would be only by playing on the 6-1. Your last bone would then have to be 4-1, 3-1, 1-1, or 1-0. He counted that if he played his 5-2 on the five, you could score 10 if you had the 4-1; if he played his bone on the 2, you could score 15 if you had the 3-1. With 1-1 or 1-0, you could not score anyway. On general principle, it would be wise to risk giving you 10 rather than 15. But here he had a sure thing. He knew you did not have the 4-1, because that is the bone he drew for first turn! (Thus you see the iniquity of drawing from the boneyard for first turn.)

HONEYMOON BRIDGE

Why You'll Like It: Honeymoon Bridge is just like the four-hand game so that you can use all your knowledge and skill in Auction or Contract Bridge to good advantage, yet different enough to create novel and exciting situations that could never otherwise arise.

What You Need: A standard 52-card pack, and pencil and paper for scoring. To save time, use two packs, each player shuffling his own pack while the other deals.

Let's Play a Game: We spread one pack and draw cards for first deal. You draw the ♠ Ace. As that is the highest card in the pack, I don't bother to show my card. Even if I drew another ace, you would win the deal, for spades are the highest suit.

You shuffle your pack, I cut it, and then you deal four hands of thirteen cards each, one at a time. Meanwhile I shuffle my pack.

We can sit opposite each other at a card table, or side

by side at a console table—it doesn't really matter. But we must agree in advance which hands we are going to pick up. We each take one hand, and the other two hands remain face down on the table. The one opposite you is your *dummy*, and the other is my *dummy*.

As dealer, you bid first. If you don't want to bid, you may pass. What you should bid on your cards depends first of all on whether we have decided to play Auction or Contract Bridge. Suppose that we have decided on Auction Bridge bidding, which makes a better game. Your hand is

In Auction Bridge you score all the tricks you make, provided that you take at least as many as you have bid. In Contract Bridge, you score only what you bid, if you make it, toward the game. If we were playing Contract, you might well open the bidding with "four spades" on your hand, for no lower contract would give you a game.

Playing Auction, you bid only "one spade." I overcall your bid with "two hearts," you bid "two spades," and I continue to bid hearts until you are pushed up to "four spades," which I "double." You pass, which *closes the auction*. Spades are the trump suit.

Having taken the bid, you are now *declarer* and I am the *defender*. Regardless of the order in which the hands were dealt, we now arrange them in the following order to the left, clockwise: declarer, defender, declarer's dummy, defender's dummy.

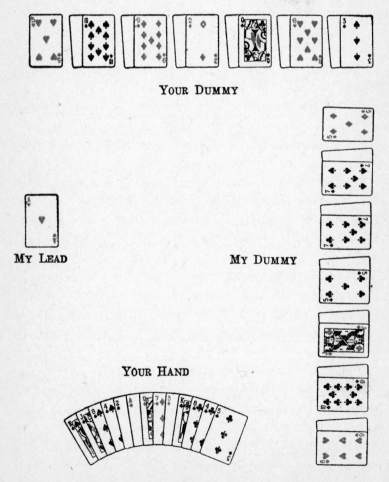

YOUR DUMMY

MY LEAD

MY DUMMY

YOUR HAND

Honeymoon Bridge

As defender, I make the *opening lead* from my own hand. Each of us then arranges his dummy. Without shuffling it, I deal the first six cards of my dummy face down in a row, then place the other seven face up, all but one of them on top of a face-down card. You do the same with your dummy.

My lead was the ♥ Ace. The cards in sight to you now are as shown in the diagram.

Your dummy plays next to the lead, and must follow suit. You play the ♥ 5 from your dummy. I follow from my dummy with the ♥ 6, and you *trump* or *ruff* the trick with the ♠ 2. You would have to play a heart if you had one, but having none you may play any card, and a trump wins a trick from a card of any other suit. You gather the four cards in a stack and put them face down on the table before you.

I now turn up the face-down card that was bared when the ♥ 6 was played off. It proves to be the ♠ Ace. You have nothing to turn up from your dummy, as the ♥ 5 was the single card.

As your hand won the trick, it makes the next lead. Seeing that the ♣ Ace is not yet in sight, you lead the ♣ 3. If I have the ♣ Ace I can win the trick, but my ♣ Ace would win a trick in any case. But if the ♣ Ace is buried in my dummy, you have sneaked by a trick with the ♣ Queen.

I follow with the ♣ 2 and the ♣ Queen does indeed win. I play the ♣ 5 from my dummy. Your dummy turns up the ♣ 9 and mine the ♥ 9. Well, this is a pleasure! You can now make your ♣ King. You lead the ♣ 9 from your dummy, bringing out the ♣ 7, ♣ King, and ♣ Jack. My dummy turns up the ♣ Ace. Too late! Now your dummy

165

shows no more clubs, and has a couple of trumps. You plan to *ruff out* your two remaining small clubs, by leading them from your hand and playing your dummy's spades on them. The appearance of the cards in sight at this juncture is shown in the diagram.

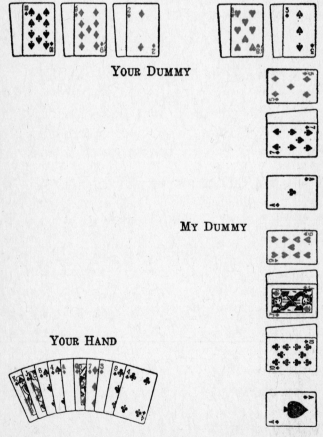

YOUR DUMMY

MY DUMMY

YOUR HAND

You lead the ♣ 4, and I play the ♠ 6. Evidently I have no trump higher than your ten in dummy, but wish to shut

out the ♠ 3. You put up the ♠ 10 and my dummy plays
the ♣ 10, being forced to follow suit to the card led. I turn
up the ♥ 3 and you turn up the ♦ 4.

Now you wish to get back to your hand in a hurry to
lead your last club. So you lead the ♥ 8, bringing out the
♥ 3, ♠ 4, and ♥ 4. Your dummy turns up the ♥ 2—you
are happy it is not a club. You lead the ♣ 8, intending to
trump with the ♠ 3, but I shut you out with the ♠ 9. From
dummy you discard the ♥ 2, thankful of the opportunity
to rid it of the suit. My dummy plays the ♣ Ace.

At this point I elect to lead a low diamond, the ♦ 6,
which brings out the ♦ 4, ♦ Jack, and ♦ Queen. But
under the ♦ Jack I find the ♠ Queen, and now your prospects are not very good against my strong trumps.

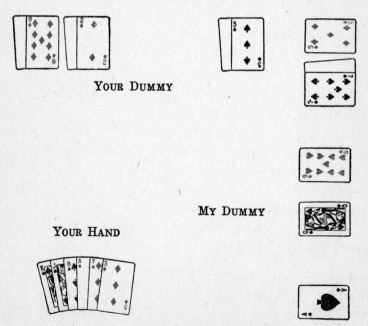

YOUR DUMMY

MY DUMMY

YOUR HAND

You cash the ♦ Ace, to which I follow with the ♦ 8, and the other hands play the ♦ 2 and ♦ 5. Under the ♦ 2 you find the ♠ 5. Having nothing better to do than hold your trumps in the hope of catching mine, you play the ♦ 3, and I win the trick with the ♦ King. Your dummy follows suit with the ♦ 9, later turning up the ♣ 6. I discard the ♥ 9 from my dummy, leaving only the three trumps showing. (Later I discover that I could have defeated you by trumping my own trick with the ♠ 7, and leading the ♠ Ace and ♠ Queen!)

Having nothing but hearts left, I lead the king. Your dummy discards the ♣ 6, and mine has to play a trump. As it certainly would be bad to play the ace, and the play of the queen does not look good, I play dummy's ♠ 7. You overtrump with the ♠ 8. To my horror, the card under the ♠ 7 is the ♦ 10. Now you can lead the ♦ 7 and trump it in your dummy with the ♠ 3, while my dummy ingloriously has to follow suit. Now on any lead from your dummy, only my ♠ Ace wins, my queen falling to your king. Thus you have lost only three tricks and have made your contract.

Even though we have agreed to play Auction Bridge in the bidding, we follow the usual practice of using the Contract Bridge scoring values. For making four odd tricks in spades, doubled, you score 240, plus a bonus of 50 points for making a doubled contract.

You have one game toward the rubber, which is the first two games out of three.

Laws of Honeymoon Bridge: *The draw.* The player drawing the higher card deals first. The cards rank: A (high), K, Q, J, 10, 9, 8, 7, 6, 5, 4, 3, 2. As between cards of the same rank, that of higher suit wins. The suits rank: Spades (high), hearts, diamonds, clubs.

Shuffle and cut. Dealer shuffles the pack to be dealt and his opponent cuts.

The deal. Four hands of thirteen cards each are dealt, one at a time. The dealer takes the hand to which the last card is dealt. Opponent takes the hand nearest himself, as determined by the seating of the two players. The remaining two hands remain face down during the auction; these are the *dummies.* If the players take adjacent hands, each takes the hand opposite himself for his dummy; if the players take alternate hands, each takes the hand on his right for his dummy.

The auction. Dealer calls first, and thereafter the players call alternately until the auction is closed. The calls are: pass, a bid, double, redouble. If dealer begins with a pass and opponent also passes, the cards are thrown in and there is a new deal by the other player. If either player makes a bid in the first round, the auction continues until one player passes, whereupon it is closed.

Each bid must name one of five declarations, ranked as follows: No trump (high), spades, hearts, diamonds, clubs. It must also name a number of *odd tricks* between one and seven inclusive. *Example:* "One heart" is a bid to win seven tricks with hearts as trumps. The odd tricks are the number beyond six which the bidder will undertake to win at his declaration.

To be legally sufficient to overcall a previous bid by opponent, a bid must name at least as many odd tricks in a declaration of higher rank, or a greater number of odd tricks. *Example:* "One diamond" overcalls "one club," but to overcall "one no trump" at least two odd tricks must be bid.

A player may double opponent's bid, or may redouble if his own bid has been doubled by opponent. Doubles and redoubles do not affect the rank of bids for overcalling sufficiency, but increase certain scoring values in the event the doubled or redoubled bid becomes the contract. A double or redouble applies only to the last preceding bid; it is voided by any succeeding bid.

The contract. The highest bid of the auction, upon its closure, becomes the *contract*, and the player who made it becomes *declarer*. His opponent is the *defender*. The four hands are then arranged in order to the left, clockwise: declarer, defender, declarer's dummy, defender's dummy.

The play. Defender makes the opening lead; he may lead any card. Each player then arranges his dummy as follows: Without shuffling, the first six cards are dealt in a row face down; the remaining seven are dealt face up, six of them upon the cards of the first row. The face-up cards are available for play; when a face-down card is bared by the play of the card above it, it is turned up and becomes available; the owner may (and should in self-interest) defer turning up such a card until the current trick is completed; he must on demand turn it up before the lead to the next trick.

Each hand plays in order clockwise, and the four cards so played constitute a *trick*. Each other hand must if able follow suit to the lead; if unable to follow suit, a hand may play any card. A trick is won by the highest trump, or if it contains no trump, by the highest card of the suit led.

HONEYMOON BRIDGE

(At no trump contracts, every trick is won by the highest card of the suit led.) The hand winning a trick leads to the next.

Each player should gather the tricks won by his hand and his dummy and place them in one overlapping line, so that the number of tricks can be seen at a glance.

Scoring. (Contract Bridge). If declarer makes at least his contract, he scores the amount of his bid *below the line* (horizontal line in the middle of the scoresheet) as follows:

DECLARATION	IF CONTRACT IS		
	UNDOUBLED	DOUBLED	REDOUBLED
No trump, for 1st odd trick	40	80	160
No trump, for each subsequent odd trick	30	60	120
Spades, for each odd trick	30	60	120
Hearts, for each odd trick	30	60	120
Diamonds, for each odd trick	20	40	80
Clubs, for each odd trick	20	40	80

The first player to amass a total of 100 or more points *below the line* wins a *game*. Both players then commence from zero score below the line upon the next game. The first player to win two games wins a *rubber*. A player who has one game toward rubber is *vulnerable*; a player with no game toward rubber is *not vulnerable*.

All scores except for odd tricks are entered *above the line*, and do not count toward game.

Any *overtricks* won by declarer in excess of his contract are scored as follows:

If the contract is undoubled, each overtrick has the same value it would have as an odd trick.

WHEN DECLARER IS	DOUBLED	REDOUBLED
Not vulnerable, each overtrick	100	200
Vulnerable, each overtrick	200	400

For making a doubled or redoubled contract, declarer scores a bonus of 50 points, regardless of vulnerability.

For bidding and making twelve tricks, *small slam*, or thirteen tricks, *grand slam*, declarer scores a premium as follows:

WHEN DECLARER IS	SMALL SLAM	GRAND SLAM
Not vulnerable	500	1000
Vulnerable	750	1500

If declarer fails to make his contract, opponent scores for *undertricks*, the tricks by which declarer falls short, as follows:

WHEN DECLARER IS	IF CONTRACT IS		
	UNDOUBLED	DOUBLED	REDOUBLED
Not vulnerable, 1st undertrick	50	100	200
Not vulnerable, each subsequent undertrick	50	200	400
Vulnerable, 1st undertrick	100	200	400
Vulnerable, each subsequent undertrick	100	300	600

When declarer fails to make contract, he may score nothing except honors, *if held*.

The *honors* at a trump declaration are the A, K, Q, J, 10 of trumps. The honors at no trump are the four aces. For holding four or five honors in his own hand or his dummy, declarer or opponent scores above the line as follows:

4 trump honors in one hand	100
5 trump honors in one hand	150
4 aces in one hand, at no trump	150

HONEYMOON BRIDGE

The player who first wins two games scores a *rubber bonus* as follows:

If opponent has won no game   700
If opponent has won one game   500

To make final settlement, all points scored by each player, both above and below the line, are totaled, and the higher total wins by the difference from the other.

Irregularities. *Irregular call.* If a call is made that is irregular for any reason, it may be voided upon demand of the opponent and the offender must substitute a regular call. If opponent makes a following call before attention is drawn to an irregular call, the latter stands as regular, and the following call, if then irregular, is void.

Lead out of turn. If a player leads when it is his opponent's turn to lead, the erroneous card must be withdrawn and there is no penalty. If a player leads from the wrong hand, as between his two hands, the error must be corrected on demand, and the player must if possible lead a card of the same suit from the right hand. In any case, if opponent follows from either hand to a lead out of turn before attention is drawn to the irregularity, the lead stands as regular.

Play out of turn. There is no penalty for playing to a trick out of turn, after a regular lead.

Dummies. Each dummy must be laid out as prescribed, after the opening lead. There is no penalty against declarer for exposing any cards of his dummy before the opening lead, but should the defender expose any card of his dummy before making the opening lead, declarer may designate the suit to be led.

Face-down cards in dummy must be turned up before the

173

lead to the next trick. They should not be turned up until the current trick is complete, but there is no penalty if a player turns up a card in his dummy after playing to the current trick from both hands. But if either player turns up a card before playing to the current trick from his own hand, his opponent may call on him to follow suit with his highest or lowest card, or to trump or discard if he has none of the suit led.

A player may spread the cards of his dummy to ascertain that the number is correct or to locate face-down cards, but may not touch the adverse dummy without permission.

Revoke. A revoke is a failure to follow suit to the lead, when able, or failure to comply with a legal penalty, when able. Any hand may correct a revoke before any cards are turned up in either dummy in consequence of the trick on which the revoke occurs, or before the lead to the next trick if no cards are to be turned. If a revoke is so corrected, cards played by the opponent to the trick after the revoke may be retracted and others substituted. If not corrected within the time limit, a revoke becomes *established* and no longer may be corrected. An established revoke by declarer or defender from his own hand is subject to penalty, as below; but neither dummy may be penalized for revoke.

In penalty for established revoke, the offender must at the end of the play give two of his tricks to his opponent for the first revoke in any suit; no penalty for any subsequent revokes in the same suit. Such transferred tricks are scored by the opponent exactly as though won in play.

Pointers on Play: If you confine your bidding to the solid values in your own hand, you will rarely score a game, for a spirited opponent will grab most of the contracts. But if you rely upon your dummy to furnish specific aces and kings, and bid accordingly, you will often take terrible beatings. You must find some reasonable middle course.

If you are familiar with Contract Bridge, you know that hand patterns are classed broadly as "defensive type" and "offensive type." The *pattern* of a hand is expressed by the numbers of cards held in each suit. The *balanced* (even) patterns: 4-3-3-3, 4-4-3-2, 5-3-3-2, 5-4-2-2, possibly 6-3-2-2, are of the "defensive type." The *unbalanced* (uneven) patterns are "offensive"; they are marked by a singleton (one card of a suit) or a void. The pattern 5-4-3-1 is mildly unbalanced, while 5-4-4-0 is strongly unbalanced and 7-4-2-0 (for example) is a "freak."

The pattern of the hand is even more significant in Honeymoon Bridge than in four-hand play. Lacking a partner to tell you what support his thirteen cards will furnish, you have to rely on abstract probability. The probability of improvement is least for a balanced hand and increases in proportion as the hand becomes more unbalanced. Therefore, with such patterns as 4-3-3-3 etc., do not bid beyond the solid values in your hand, while such patterns as 5-4-3-1, 6-4-2-1, rely on your dummy for a trick or two, and with 5-4-4-0, etc. expect dummy to give two to four tricks.

The pattern, however, is only one of two primary factors. The other is the number and distribution of high cards. Manifestly, distributed high cards have more "places open" for improvement than massed high cards. Compare the two hands in the diagram.

♠ A K Q J 4   ♠ Q J 6 4 3
♥ 9 8 7 6   ♥ K 9 8 7
♦ 10 3 2   ♦ A 10 2
♣ 5   ♣ 5

The first hand, destitute of tops outside of spades, has little prospect of improvement. Any high cards in dummy will have to function on their own merits, for the hand has no supporting honors. The second hand, with distributed values, has considerable prospects of any improvement. Any card as good as a jack, in spades, hearts, or diamonds, turned up in dummy, will strengthen and be strengthened by this hand.

For example, turn back to your hand in the illustrative game.

The strong pattern and excellent distribution of top cards warrant an opening bid of four spades. Now exchange the ♠ 2 for the ♠ Ace and the ♦ Ace for the ♦ 2, and the hand is not nearly so good. A bid of four spades would still be a good speculation, but the chances of making it are, in the abstract, considerably less.

A secondary reason why distribution of high cards is desirable is that it gives greater prospect of capturing the lead from the defender quickly. Many shaky contracts are makable if declarer can get in at once and sneak some tricks in before the full strength of the defender's dummy becomes available.

The play of the cards is grounded upon the play of four-hand Bridge. Space does not permit us to treat this very extensive subject in detail; we will only point out the possibilities peculiar to Honeymoon Bridge.

HONEYMOON BRIDGE

In four-hand Bridge, declarer's proper course in the majority of trump declarations is to lead trumps early, so as to take out the adverse trumps that might otherwise ruff his side tricks. But in Honeymoon Bridge, the occasions for deferring trump leads are so numerous and frequent that this campaign is the exception rather than the rule.

In the first place, if the defender's dummy shows no trumps, there is scarcely virtue in leading trumps, so as to pull one from defender's hand for each two from the declarer's cards. In the second place, the dummies very often are such as to make certain other plays immediately imperative, before the turn of additional cards spoils the opportunity. We have seen two such plays in the illustrative game—the ruffing of losing plain cards by declarer's dummy, temporarily void of the plain (non-trump) suit; the sneaking through of a high-card trick before the ace of the suit turns up in the defender's dummy. Another type of "rush job" is the slaughter of an unguarded honor in the adverse dummy, before saving guards turn up.

With a choice of play in following suit from dummy, between a single card and another that covers a buried card, consider whether at this juncture you wish to bring a new card into play. Sometimes you will not want to do so; for example, when you plan to use dummy trumps for ruffing. And there are subtle occasions when you pray for a specific card to turn up in your dummy but don't want it too soon. For example, you have contracted at no trump, having stoppers in three suits, but only small cards in hearts. The defender opens the ace of hearts, and your dummy fails to show a stopper in hearts. The correct play from dummy is the single card, if you can spare it. Your only hope is that your dummy will turn up a heart stopper, but if it turns up too soon, it may be dropped by the defender's top cards. A singleton jack or ten in your dummy may eventually stop the suit, provided that it doesn't turn up until the defender has cashed all his higher hearts.

Conversely, occasions arise when it is imperative to uncover new cards as quickly as possible. You may need to find a high card to support a lead from your hand toward the dummy, in a suit in which the adverse dummy at your right has a high card. Or you may need to find out exactly what is against you, in order to know how to manipulate a key suit. Look also for possible advantage from forcing the play of covering cards from the adverse dummy, to bring buried cards in sight. This course is a frequent defense against ruffs by the adverse dummy.

There is less difference between the play by the defender and by the declarer in Honeymoon Bridge than in four-hand Bridge. All the strategy of declarer's play is equally available to the defender, except that he is usually less prepared to lead trumps to advantage, and consequently has a greater interest in making trumps by ruffing.

It is of course vital to keep track of all the cards as played, to note what cards are yet to be disclosed, and to make inferences as to the opponent's holding from his play. This department of the game is the same as in four-hand Bridge, with one added element of uncertainty. Inferences from the adverse play must reckon with the opponent's uncertainty as to the full contents of his dummy, so long as any card is still buried.

GLOSSARY

AT HOME (*Cribbage*), having a total score as good as average expectancy.

AVAILABLE CARD (*Russian Bank*), one that can be moved elsewhere.

BACK DOOR (*Bezique*), a sequence in a non-trump suit.

BACKGAMMON (*Backgammon*), winning of a game when the opponent still has a stone in the winner's home table or on the bar.

BALKING CARDS (*Cribbage*), those which, laid in the crib, have the least chance of making scoring combinations.

BAR (*Backgammon*), the division between the inner and outer tables.

BEAR OFF (*Backgammon*), remove stones from play, after all have reached one's own home table.

BELLA (*Kalabrias*), the king and queen of trumps held by one hand, when announced for a score.

BETE (pronounced bate) (*Kalabrias*), forfeit suffered for losing in play.

BEZIQUE (*Bezique*), a declaration comprising a queen of trumps and a certain jack of opposite color.

BIG CASINO (*Casino*), the ◇ 10.

BLANK CARD, the only one of its suit held in the hand.

BLOCK (*Mill*), occupy a point to prevent the opponent from taking it and making a mill. (*Sniff*), an impasse in which neither hand can play and the boneyard is exhausted.

BONE (*Sniff*), any domino.

BONEYARD (*Sniff*), the rest of the dominoes, after the original hands are drawn.

BOX (*Gin Rummy*), a bonus for winning a deal, awarded at the end of a game.

BUILD (*Casino*), put two or more cards in a pile and announce the rank of the card with which they can be taken in.

CARTE BLANCHE (*Bezique*), a hand with no face card (king, queen or jack.)

CASH POINTS (*Casino*), cards of intrinsic rather than contributory value: aces, big casino, little casino.

CENTER (*Russian Bank*), the foundations collectively.

CLOSE A MILL (*Mill*), move a piece onto a line to make three-in-a-row.

COMFORT STATION (*Backgammon*), the adverse 12-point.

COVER (*Backgammon*), make a point by placing a second stone on a blot.

CRIB (*Cribbage*), the extra hand of four cards formed by the discards.

CUT, divide the pack into two packets and place the former bottom pack on top.

DEADWOOD (*Gin Rummy*), unmatched cards, collectively.

DECLARATION (*Bezique*), a combination of cards of scoring value.

DECLARE (*Bezique*), place a declaration on the table.

DISCARD, throw cards out of the hand; delete cards from the pack for certain games; play a non-trump card when unable to follow suit to a lead.

DIX (pronounced deece) (*Kalabrias*), the lowest trump in the pack. (*Pinochle*), the 9 of trumps.

DOUBLE (*Backgammon*), a demand that the value of the game be doubled if the opponent chooses to play on.

DOUBLE MILL (*Mill*), a formation in which one piece moves between two points, closing a mill in each turn.

DOUBLE PAIR ROYAL (*Cribbage*), four of a kind.

DRAW, obtain additional cards, at some period after the deal; take a card from the pack before the deal, to determine the dealer, precedence, etc.

DROP (*Backgammon*), resign the game when opponent doubles.

END (*Sniff*), one of the two numbers on a bone.

ENTER (*Backgammon*), bring a stone from the bar into the adverse home table.

GLOSSARY

FIFTEEN (*Cribbage*), any combination of two or more cards totaling 15 in pips.

FLUSH (*Pinochle*), a meld of the A-K-Q-J-10 of trumps. (*Cribbage*), four or five of the same suit.

FOLLOW SUIT, play a card of the same suit as the lead to a trick.

FORK (*Mill*), play so as to threaten to make a mill on either of two intersecting lines.

FOUNDATION (*Russian Bank*), an ace and all cards built on it.

GAMMON (*Backgammon*), winning of a game when the opponent has not borne off a single stone.

GIN HAND (*Gin Rummy*), one with no unmatched card.

GO (*Cribbage*), call by a player indicating that he cannot play another card without exceeding 31.

GOOD (*Kalabrias*), concession by a player that a sequence announced by opponent is entitled to score.

GROUP (*Gin Rummy*), a set of three or four of a kind, as distinguished from a sequence.

HAND (*Russian Bank*), the rest of the pack after the layout is dealt.

HEAVY (*Sniff*), of higher number; having a larger total of pips.

HIS HEELS (*Cribbage*), a jack in the crib.

HIS NOBS (*Cribbage*), a jack turned as starter.

HIT (*Backgammon*), place a stone on a point occupied by an adverse blot.

HOME TABLE (*Backgammon*), inner table.

INNER TABLE (*Backgammon*), that half of the board containing the points numbered from 1 to 6.

JASZ (pronounced yahss), (*Kalabrias*), the jack of trumps.

KNOCK (*Gin Rummy*), place the hand face up on the table, ending the play.

LAY AWAY (*Cribbage*), discard to the crib.

LAY OFF (*Gin Rummy*), add a matching card to a set laid down by the knocker.

LAYOUT (*Russian Bank*), the cards dealt to begin a game, comprising tableau and stock. (*Sniff*), the bones already played on the table, collectively (also called tableau).

LIGHT (*Sniff*), of lower number; having a lower total of pips.

LINE (*Gin Rummy*), same as BOX.

LITTLE CASINO (*Casino*), the ♠ 2.

LOAD (*Russian Bank*), build cards on the adverse stock or talon.

LOVER'S LEAP (*Backgammon*), the move of a runner from adverse 1-point to 12-point, on roll of 6-5.

LURCH (*Cribbage*), failure of the loser of a game to reach the half-total of points necessary to win.

MAKE A POINT (*Backgammon*), place two or more stones on a point.

MAKER (*Kalabrias*), the player held responsible by rule for naming the trump suit.

MARRIAGE (*Pinochle, Bezique*), a meld or declaration of a king and queen of the same suit.

MELD (*Pinochle*), a combination of cards of scoring value; place a meld on the table.

MENEL (*Kalabrias*) (pronounced muh-NELL), the 9 of trumps.

MILL (*Mill*), three pieces of the same color on a line of the board.

MISDEAL, a deal which violates a rule of correct procedure.

MISS (*Backgammon*), fail to roll a desired number.

MUGGINS (*Cribbage, Sniff*), the right of a player to score points overlooked by his opponent.

NATURAL (*Sniff*), a bone, the sum or difference of whose ends is 5 or 10; any bone of intrinsic value.

NEAR CARDS (*Cribbage*), those close but not adjacent in rank.

ON THE BAR (*Backgammon*), having a stone that must be entered, after it has been hit as a blot.

OPEN A MILL (*Mill*), move a piece off the line of a mill.

OPEN END (*Sniff*), a branch of the layouts on which it is legal to play.

OUTER TABLE (*Backgammon*), that half of the board containing the points numbered 7 to 12.

GLOSSARY

PEG (*Cribbage*), a scoring implement; to mark a score on the cribbage board.

PINOCHLE (*Pinochle*), a meld of ♠ Q and ◇ J.

PLACES OPEN (*Gin Rummy*), specific cards that will complete sets in the hand if drawn.

PLAY OFF (*Cribbage*), play a card wide in rank from the previous card.

PLAY ON (*Cribbage*), play one near in rank to the previous card.

POINT (*Mill*), any of the 24 intersections on the board. (*Backgammon*), any of the 24 marks on the board on which the stones are placed and moved.

PRIME (*Backgammon*), six adjacent points made by one player.

RENEGE (pronounced ree-NIG), same as REVOKE.

REVOKE, fail to follow suit when required by rule to do so; commit an irregularity for which the same penalty is applied as for a revoke.

RUBICON (*Bezique*), failure of the loser of a game to reach 3,000 points.

RUN (*Cribbage*), three or more cards in sequence.

RUNNER (*Backgammon*), a stone in the adverse home table.

SCHMEISS (*Kalabrias*), a proposal to abandon the cards and have a new deal.

SEQUENCE, three or more cards of adjacent rank in the same suit. (*Bezique*), the five highest cards of a suit.

SET, three or four cards of the same rank, or three or more cards in sequence in the same suit.

SHOW (*Cribbage*), count the hands and crib after the play.

SHUTOUT (*Gin Rummy*), a failure of the loser of a game to win a single point. (*Backgammon*), a prime in the home table.

SPACE (*Russian Bank*), a vacancy created by clearing away one of the eight piles of the tableau.

STARTER (*Rummy*), a card turned from the top of the stock after the deal to start the discard pile. (*Cribbage*), a card cut from the stock by non-dealer.

STOCK, a reserve of undealt cards.

STONE (*Backgammon*), any of the pieces with which the game is played.

STOP (*Russian Bank*), a call upon opponent to cease play, in penalty for violating a rule of procedure.

SUIT (*Sniff*), all the bones having a common end.

SWEEP (*Casino*), the taking in of all cards on the table.

TABLEAU (*Russian Bank*), eight cards dealt face up in the layout, with all other cards built upon them.

TAKE (*Kalabrias*), accept the turned up card for trump.

TAKE IN (*Casino*), capture one or more cards from the table with a card from the hand.

TALON (*Russian Bank*), waste pile of unplayable cards turned up from the hand.

TENTH CARD (*Cribbage*), one whose pip count is 10, any face card or ten-spot.

TRAIL (*Casino*), play a card to the table without taking in.

TRUMP CARD (*Pinochle*), the next card of the pack after the deal, turned to fix the trump suit.

UNDERCUT (*Gin Rummy*), have as low or a lower count of deadwood than the opponent after he knocks.

UNLOAD (*Rummy*), lay sets on the table.

UNMATCHED CARD (*Gin Rummy*), one that is not part of a set.

UPCARD (*Gin Rummy*), a card turned up from the stock after the deal to start the discard pile; the top card of the discard pile. (*Ed. note.* The laws define the term in the first sense and use it in the second.)

WIDE CARDS (*Cribbage*), those far apart in rank.

WILD CARD, one which can be designated as of any suit and rank, at the pleasure of the holder.